G000134784

The Antarctic circumpolar ocean

Studies in Polar Research

This series of publications reflects the growth of research activity in and about the polar regions, and provides a means of disseminating the results. Coverage is international and interdisciplinary: the books will be relatively short (about 200 pages), but fully illustrated. Most will be surveys of the present state of knowledge in a given subject rather than research reports, conference proceedings or collected papers. The scope of the series is wide and will include studies in all the biological, physical and social sciences.

Edited by

R. J. Adie, British Antarctic Survey, Cambridge

T. E. Armstrong (chairman), Scott Polar Research Institute, Cambridge

S. W. Greene, Department of Botany, University of Reading

B. Stonehouse, Scott Polar Research Institute, Cambridge

P. Wadhams, Scott Polar Research Institute, Cambridge

P. N. Webb, Department of Geology and Mineralogy, Ohio State University

I. Whitaker, Department of Anthropology, Simon Fraser University, British Columbia

The first titles in this series will be:

The Antarctic Circumpolar Ocean
Sir George Deacon

Antarctic Birds
The History and Literature of Antarctic Ornithology
The late Brian B. Roberts
Edited by B. Stonehouse *Scott Polar Research Institute, Cambridge*

Life of the Tundra
Yw. I. Chernov

The Antarctic circumpolar ocean

GEORGE DEACON

Formerly, Director of the Institute of Oceanographic Sciences

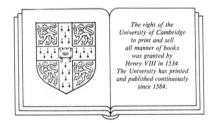

*The right of the
University of Cambridge
to print and sell
all manner of books
was granted by
Henry VIII in 1534.
The University has printed
and published continuously
since 1584.*

CAMBRIDGE UNIVERSITY PRESS

Cambridge

London New York New Rochelle

Melbourne Sydney

Published by the Press Syndicate of the University of Cambridge
The Pitt Building, Trumpington Street, Cambridge CB2 1RP
32 East 57th Street, New York, NY 10022, USA
296 Beaconsfield Parade, Middle Park, Melbourne 3206, Australia

© Cambridge University Press 1984

First published 1984

Printed in Great Britain at the University Press, Cambridge

Library of Congress catalogue card number: 83–26332

British Library cataloguing in publication data
Deacon, *Sir* George
The Antarctic circumpolar ocean.
1. Antarctic Ocean
I. Title
909'.90670828   GC461
ISBN 0 521 25410 8

Contents

Preface This book is planned as one of a series to reflect growing interest in polar research, and while suitable for a wider readership is largely intended for students moving into oceanography or polar studies from other scientific backgrounds. The first part deals with the early ideas and evidence of a great southern continent, the pioneering observations of the early explorers and of the sealers who profited from the new discoveries, the observations made by polar explorers on their way to the continent, and the systematic studies of oceanographic expeditions. The second part summarizes present knowledge of the water movements and their probable effects on temperature and salinity distributions, biological productivity, distributions of marine plants and animals, climate and ice cover. It tries to show how the present knowledge has grown from earlier findings, and to indicate its relevance to economic problems, such as the conservation of marine living resources.

In this broad account it seemed better to use familiar units as used by the original observers and more likely than new specialist notations to present a lively picture.

I am indebted to Dr Peter Wadhams of the Scott Polar Research Institute, to Dr Nigel Bonner of the British Antarctic Survey and to Dr Arthur Baker and the librarians of the Institute of Oceanographic

Sciences for their help, and to Cambridge University Press and particularly Mrs Karin Fancett the subeditor who suggested many improvements to the manuscript.

I am grateful to the Institute of Oceanographic Sciences for the photographs, formerly the property of the Discovery Committee and the National Institute of Oceanography. The photographs of Grytviken and the Blue Whale were taken by the late Dr N. A. Mackintosh, and the others by the late Dr E. H. Marshall, surgeon in the *Discovery* and *Discovery II* till 1931, and by the late A. Saunders FRPS on the later voyages. Those of the RRS *William Scoresby*, the Fur Seal and HMS *Ajax* were taken by myself.

Introduction Captain Cook, impressed by the uniformity of climate, winds, currents and marine life all round the Antarctic, used the collective name Southern Ocean for the circumpolar ring of water. Antarctic Ocean is also used, though mainly for the southern part, south of the Antarctic convergence, where, as will be shown later, cold water typical of the icy regime farther south begins to sink below warmer water. Hydrographic offices needing precise divisions do not use the name Southern Ocean, though they publish Antarctic Pilots – sailing directions for the land and islands south of the usual route of vessels. For political reasons the governments of Argentina and Chile emphasize separation rather than continuity between the Atlantic and Pacific Oceans, and the Inter-governmental Oceanographic Commission of UNESCO has to write Southern Oceans in the plural. US scientists were advised to spell it without capital letters.

Since the early voyages round Cape Horn and Captain Cook's circumnavigation, the Southern Ocean has become notorious for strong winds, high seas and danger from ice. Its seals and whales have been the source of enormous wealth, and now its shrimp-like krill, on which much of the Antarctic life depends, is itself being exploited. Before the opening of the Suez and Panama Canals the Antarctic circumpolar ocean was one of the principal trade routes and it is increasingly used for

1

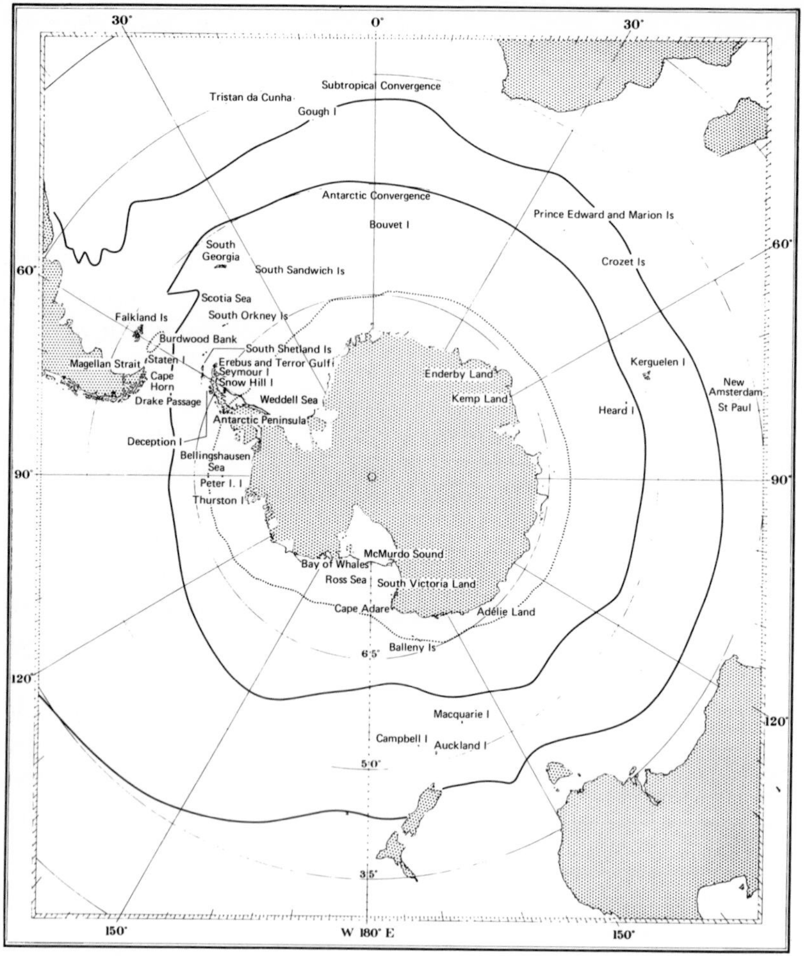

Figure 1
The Antarctic circumpolar ocean and the
Antarctic and subtropical convergences

access to the continent. It exerts great influence on the climates of the neighbouring continents and oceans. Its main geographical features are shown in Figure 1.

The early explorers The Greeks and Romans, convinced that the earth was round, wondered what was on the other side. Encouraged by Ptolemy, the Alexandrian astronomer, the idea grew that there must be a southern continent to balance the northern land masses. By the Middle Ages, it had advanced to speculation as to whether people lived there, and whether profit could be gained from it. Sixteenth-century maps show a large circumpolar continent extending to the Magellan Strait, to the dimly-known northern extremity of Australia, and separated from the better-known East Indies by only a narrow strait. Bartolomeu Dias and Vasco da Gama had long before opened up the sea route from Europe to the East round the Cape of Good Hope. Drake pushed back the possible limits of the continent in 1578, when, driven to the south-east after passing through the Magellan Strait, he found the southern tip of South America in about 56° S. Beyond this he could see only open ocean. Isaac le Maire, a Dutch merchant, and William Schouten, his captain, were the first to enter the Pacific Ocean through this opening, now called the Drake Passage, in 1616. Le Maire named the southernmost cape after the town of Hoorn, and land to the east, seen as they passed through a narrow strait, the Le Maire Strait; they called Staten Land after their parliament. They believed it to be part of the southern continent, but it was shown to be an island by another Dutch seaman, Hendrik Brouwer, in 1643. On the other side of the world more ocean was opened when Abel Tasman sailed south of Australia and Tasmania in 1642. The rich

3

literature discussing these early voyages is attractively summarized by the late Professor J. C. Beaglehole in his introduction to *The Journals of Captain Cook, The Voyage of the* Endeavour, *1768–1771*, published by the Hakluyt Society and Cambridge University Press, in 1955.

The first deliberate attempt to sail far south seems to be that of the astronomer Edmond Halley, when he sailed to within about 100 nautical miles of South Georgia in the small naval vessel *Paramore* only 52 feet long, in January 1700. His main purpose was the mapping of magnetic variation, but he had also been instructed by the Admiralty to explore the coast of Terra Incognita, believed to lie between the Magellan Strait and the Cape of Good Hope. He found the southern waters very cold and inhospitable compared with similar northern latitudes. In $52\frac{1}{2}°$ S he 'fell in with great Islands of Ice, of soe Incredible a hight and magnitude, that I scarce dare write my thoughts of it, at first we took it for land with chaulky cliffs, and the top all covered with snow, but we soon found our mistake by standing in with it, and that it was nothing but ice, though it could not be less than 200 foot high and one island at least 5 mile in front'. Seeing penguins made him think he was near land, but the bad weather, imminent danger of being drifted on to the ice, and failure to get any sight of the sun that would allow him to fix his magnetic observations, made him retreat.

The next to encounter Antarctic icebergs was Jacob Roggeveen, an explorer sponsored by the Dutch East India Company. Sailing in 1721 he touched at the Falkland Islands and then sailed beyond 60° S to secure his passage round the Horn. He saw innumerable icebergs which he took as evidence of a continent farther south; he thought it might, like Greenland, be inhabited by fishermen. The next discovery was on New Year's Day 1739, when a French captain, Bouvet de Lozier, found an icy cape near 54° S south-west of the Cape of Good Hope. Because of the date he called it Cape Circumcision. Bad weather prevented closer and fuller investigation, and he left after ten days thinking it was part of the southern continent. In January 1771 Marc Macé Marion du Fresne, a French explorer on his way to Tasmania and New Zealand, sighted the steep, cloud-capped islands now called Marion and Prince Edward Islands, some 900 nautical miles south-east of Cape Town. He called the larger island Terre d'Esperance, hoping that the continent was close by; but his ships had been damaged in collision, and he did not want to get involved with ice farther south, so turned eastwards. Ten days later he saw the Crozet Islands, so named by Captain Cook a few years later after du Fresne's second in command.

In February 1772 Yves Joseph de Kerguelen-Trémarec, a Breton nobleman and adventurer, sighted the island that now bears his name. He did little to examine it, but took home a preposterous story of a Southern France, part of the southern continent, able to produce all the crops grown in the same northern latitudes, and rich minerals besides. Sailing again in 1773 he traded at Mauritius and Cape Town, but took little interest in his new discovery; during 34 days spent there little was achieved, he never landed himself or showed that it was an island, though appropriately he renamed it Land of Desolation, an epithet used by Cook after he examined the island in 1776. It was afterwards used by sealers and whalers, and by German commerce raiders in World War II. France now maintains a station there and leases fishing rights round the islands.

There were two British circumnavigations during the period 1764 to 1769 but they did not venture into high latitudes. The first was led by Commodore John Byron, who had been midshipman in the *Wager*,

Anson's ship that was wrecked north of the western end of the Magellan Strait. His instructions included searching for lands and islands of great extent hitherto unvisited by any European power, which there was reason to believe might be found in the Atlantic Ocean between the Cape of Good Hope and the Magellan Strait, within latitudes convenient for navigation and in climates adapted to the produce of commodities useful in commerce. Captains Samuel Wallis, who had sailed with Byron, and Philip Carteret were given similar instructions two years later, and told to search westwards from Cape Horn, standing as far south as possible to look for lands believed to lie in that part of the Southern Hemisphere. Byron did useful work in the Falkland Islands, though he missed seeing a thriving French settlement at Port Louis. They both felt obliged to turn north-west in the Pacific Ocean, adding to the geography of the tropical islands, and Wallis discovered Tahiti. It is perhaps remarkable that these eminent professionals seem not to have been able to face the conditions that Halley had endured and Cook was soon to master; perhaps it was fear of scurvy.

Science, industry and national interests had much in common in the golden days of exploration, and Cook's voyages were helped and partly originated by the Royal Society's campaign for south-sea observations of the 1769 Transit of Venus, to advance astronomical theory and better determination of the distance of the earth from the sun. Except for reaching 60° S south-west of Cape Horn, the first voyage was in relatively low latitudes, but its discoveries, surveys, magnetic and gravity measurements, studies of climate, winds, tides and currents, impressive natural history collections, paintings and sketches, and novel information about native peoples and their way of life, promoted public interest in scientific exploration. Cook himself said that the question of

Figure 2
Pedro Sound, leading southwards from the Magellan Strait, 24 October 1934

the southern continent, which had been the object of many ages and nations should be the aim of another voyage farther south: there was little hope of finding it north of 40° S. In the meantime Alexander Dalrymple, well informed on the early voyages and enthusiastic proponent of a large, populous continent in the south Pacific, had published his two-volume *Historical Collection of the Several Voyages in the South Pacific Ocean*, continuing to maintain the existence of a southern continent. It roused public interest, and probably helped to promote the second voyage.

During this voyage (1772–75), Cook in the *Resolution* and Tobias Furneaux in the *Adventure* sailed south from Cape Town finding the air becoming 'pinching cold' in 48° S, near the Antarctic convergence, and seeing their first iceberg in 51° S. They were stopped in 55° S by an immense ice field to which there seemed no end. This was 14 December, and we now know that in early summer there are two zones of pack ice in these longitudes, an outer tongue moving eastwards from the northern margin of the Weddell Sea and, much farther south, a continuous zone of ice along the margin of the Antarctic continent. Between them the ice melts in early summer. Cook followed the northern tongue as far as 31° E, and was then able to round it and steer south and then south-west into the open water. In 60° S he was able to reach 10° E, well beyond the longitude in which he first met the ice in 55° S, and also beyond the longitude in which Bouvet's Cape Circumcision had been charted. Seeing no land, and considering the tasks that lay ahead, he turned back to the east. His journal suggests that he would have liked to sail farther west to find the land from which, he supposed, the ice to the north of him must be coming, but there was no time.

After taking up as much ice as the ships could hold, from the loose bits broken from an iceberg, to be melted for drinking water, they turned south in 40° E and crossed the Antarctic Circle, approximately $66\frac{1}{2}$° S, on 17 January. They were the first ships to cross it. They met the coastal pack-ice zone in 67°15′ S, observations from the mast head showing nothing but ice from E to WSW. Here Cook was only 75 nautical miles from the coast of what, 58 years later, was sighted and called Enderby Land. He then turned north-east to sail south of the Crozets and Kerguelen, showing that they were not part of a continent. Here the *Adventure* became separated from the *Resolution*. The *Adventure* continued her way eastwards to Tasmania and New Zealand; sailing mainly between 51° S and 53° S she experienced a constant succession of strong west winds, while Cook, some 8 to 10 degrees farther south had more variable weather, with some east winds and calm spells. Meeting icebergs south of 57° S, he reached 61°52′ S in 95°15′ E. Here he found navigation very difficult because of bad weather among a great number of icebergs and large pieces broken from them, and could not cross the Antarctic Circle again as he hoped. He continued eastwards in about 60° S as far as the longitude of Tasmania, and then turned north-east to New Zealand.

After more surveys among the Pacific islands Cook turned south again at the end of November. He sailed alone; the *Adventure*, having failed to rendezvous in New Zealand, sailed home via Cape Horn and Cape Town. Cook crossed the Antarctic Circle again on 21 December and was stopped by pack ice in 67°19′ S, 138°15′ W, thick ice floes stretching over the whole sea. On 26 December the *Resolution* was drifting among many icebergs, upwards of 200 being visible within a compass of 5 miles, besides innumerable smaller pieces. Faced with such difficulties and the desirability of filling in a great blank farther north Cook then made a search as far as 48° S between 140° W and 110° W. At about the same time Furneaux in the *Adventure* was crossing the ocean in approximately 60° S. To the disappointment of the sailors, who thought they were going home, Cook again turned south and crossed the Antarctic Circle for the third time on 26 January. A few days later, on 30 January 1774, he reached his farthest south, 71°10′ S in 106°54′ W. He mentions an immense ice field, with broken ice so compact that nothing could enter it, and a solid body of ice a mile or so beyond. He remarked on the brightness of the horizon: the clouds appearing white as snow in the light reflected from the ice – afterwards known as ice blink. From here, convinced of the improbability of finding land in these high latitudes so late in the season, he turned northwards to the Tropics, through a region where Dalrymple thought the reports of earlier voyages gave some evidence of undiscovered land. Nothing was found, but they enjoyed a visit to Easter Island, and, probably with more disappointment to the sailors, sailed back to the west, adding much to the geography of the tropical islands, and reaching New Zealand again after discovering New Caledonia and Norfolk Islands.

Less than a month later they were at sea again, crossing the Pacific Ocean in 55–60° S to be in good time to investigate the Atlantic sector. Reaching South America near the western end of the Magellan Strait, Cook made a running survey of the west and south coasts of Tierra del Fuego, naming a number of the prominent features, spending a week in Christmas Sound, and celebrating the third Christmas of the voyage with the mussels, ducks, shags, geese and wild celery, that were found there. In the Atlantic Ocean he examined Staten Island and, after looking in vain for a coastline surmised by Dalrymple, found South

Georgia. He surveyed the north-east coast, landing in Possession Bay. He thought he might have found a tip of the southern continent, but rounding the eastern end of the island he could see the south-west coast stretching back, obviously to the point where he had first seen the island six days earlier. He named the south-eastern point Cape Disappointment, but wrote that he was not very disappointed for if the continent was anything like this sample it would not be worth discovering. He named it Isle of Georgia, and wondered that it should, in only 54–55° S latitude, be covered by so much snow and ice in the middle of summer. A week later he discovered the South Sandwich Islands. In the prevailing bad weather, and not being able to anchor near such steep coasts, he could not be sure whether all of them were islands, but the points he named have since been found to be charted with remarkable accuracy. The last one he saw, though since found not to be the northernmost of the group, was sighted on 2 February and called Candlemas. After this another search was made for Bouvet's Cape Circumcision before they sailed home. It is almost incredible what they had been through.

Cook's instructions for this voyage had laid considerable emphasis on scientific studies. The Board of Longitude, the commissioners appointed by Parliament to promote more accuracy in measurements of longitude at sea, found him two astronomers. William Wales, who had worked on the *Nautical Almanac*, and had observed the 1769 Transit of Venus at Hudson Bay, sailed with Cook in the *Resolution*. William Bayly, an assistant at the Royal Observatory who had observed the Transit at North Cape, sailed with Furneaux in the *Adventure*. One of their main tasks was exhaustive checking of the chronometers recently developed to carry Greenwich time, so that longitude could be measured from the

difference between local time, from sun sights, and Greenwich time. The checking was done by comparing the chronometer times with figures obtained from the difference between local measurements of the angular distance of the moon from the sun, or from a fixed star, and corresponding angles predicted for Greenwich, newly available in tables. It required considerable skill in observation and computation, and having such expertise always at hand must have been a great help to Cook, enabling him to be certain of measuring longitude to within $1\frac{1}{2}$ degrees, and generally to within $\frac{1}{2}$ degree. In the course of his careful work Wales found that compass variations calculated from bearings of the sun when it was on one side of the ship often differed from those obtained when it was on the other side. Cook and the ship's officers were not very interested, calling Wales a philosopher, but after that the journal often gave two slightly different values for the variation. The cause of the differences was not fully understood till Matthew Flinders, 50 years later, demonstrated the collective effect of a ship's iron on the compass, deflecting it one way on one heading, and the other way on the opposite heading.

Wales and Bayly were also instructed to measure air and sea temperatures, and to lower thermometers to great depths as opportunity occurred. They managed to make only nine deep observations, all of them during the first six months, so that it could not have been considered very important. Those they did make showed that in the Antarctic region there was warmer water, at 100 fathoms or so, below the cold surface layer, whereas farther north the temperature decreased continuously with depth. We now know that the Antarctic surface layer has a lower salt content, which, in spite of its low temperature, makes it lighter than the warmer, but more saline, water that is spreading

Figure 3
Saunders Island, South Sandwich Islands, 17 March 1930

13

southwards below it. There is no record of Wales and Bayly trying to measure salinity, though they are supposed to have had a water sampler. Perhaps they lost it, because when they were finally on the way home in 1775 Anders Sparrman, the Swedish naturalist who had helped Reinhold and George Forster, the official naturalists, throughout the voyage, improvised a sampler and collected samples for Torbern Bergman, one of the first chemists to analyse sea water.

Cook reached sound conclusions about the origin of the icebergs so frequently encountered. His observations at South Georgia convinced him that the valleys of a continent farther south must be filled by a great depth of everlasting snow, terminating in big ice cliffs at the sea. The vast quantity of ice he saw made him believe that such cliffs must sometimes extend far into the sea, and break off to produce icebergs. Where they occurred seaward of wide valleys they would produce the big tabular icebergs. They were formed, he concluded, by snow continually falling or drifting down from the mountains.

The Forsters, father and son, were taken on at short notice because Banks and his helpers, who had done such good work during Cook's earlier voyage in the *Endeavour*, would not sail without better accommodation. Reinhold Forster was a very learned man, with wide experience in natural history, but he proved an unusually complaining and unadaptable shipmate, and George naturally took his father's part. They made careful botanical and zoological studies, and were very interested in the way of life, religions and languages of the Pacific islanders, but failed to rouse such enthusiasm and public interest as that earned by Banks and his colleagues in the *Endeavour*.

The main results of the voyage were the surveys and charts, all the information on tides, currents, winds, weather and climate, and the demonstration that there must be a frozen continent to produce so much ice, though it must for the most part lie south of the Antarctic Circle, and be inaccessible to ordinary shipping. Another great result was Cook's clear demonstration that such long voyages could be made without any trouble from scurvy. For this triumph he was awarded the Royal Society's Copley Medal. He proved the reliability of the new timekeepers in all the vicissitudes experienced in small ships on difficult voyages. His reports of an abundance of seals and whales soon brought many ships to Antarctic waters.

The sealers   Within three years of Cook's landing on South Georgia, British sealers were at work there. They were soon followed by Americans, and by the time James Weddell arrived there in 1823, the Fur Seals, valued for their skins, and the Elephant Seals valued for their oil, were almost extinct. He estimated that 1 200 000 skins and 20 000 tons of oil had been taken. In the meantime sealing had spread to other parts of the circumpolar ocean. Hugh Robert Mill, in his *Siege of the South Pole* deduced that by 1791 no less than 102 ships averaging 200 tons, manned by 3000 seamen, were fur and elephant sealing in the Southern Ocean, the majority at South Georgia and in the Magellan Strait. A tremendous slaughter took place in the South Shetland Islands immediately after their discovery by William Smith in 1819. When he arrived there in the 1821–22 season, he found himself in company with 15 to 20 British ships and 30 American, so that during the fishing season it was difficult to maintain peace between crews of the two nations who were on shore. Weddell estimated that 320 000 Fur Seals were killed in the 1821–22 season. Even ships from Hobart and Sydney joined in, and the seals

Figure 4
A Fur Seal on Bird Island, South Georgia,
23 October 1936

were practically wiped out. W. H. B. Webster, surgeon in HMS *Chanticleer*, in his account of her voyage to the South Shetlands in 1829, wrote 'The harvest of the sea has been so effectually reaped, that not a single Fur Seal was seen by us during our visit to the South Shetland Group; and, although it is but a few years back since countless multitudes covered the shores, the ruthless spirit of barbarism slaughtered young and old alike, so as to destroy the race. Formerly two thousand skins a week could be procured by a vessel; now not a single seal is to be seen.'

The destruction of seals at Macquarie Island, on the other side of the world, is another example of the ruthless intensity with which the sealers pursued their trade; but in some out-of-the-way inaccessible sites the seals lived on, and, after being left in comparative peace for 50 years, began to multiply afresh. HMS *Challenger* found sealers taking about 100 in one day at Kerguelen in 1874, but only 33 000 skins could be secured from various parts of the South Shetland Islands in 20 years, between 1871 and 1891. From this second onslaught, recovery was slower; 17 years later an American sealer found only 39 seals, and the Swedish South Polar Expedition, covering a wide area, including South Georgia and the South Shetlands in 1901–03, saw only one. In 1927 a party from the *Norvegia* found a small colony on Bouvet Island, and George Rayner of the Discovery Investigations saw a few stragglers on Bird Island, near the northern tip of South Georgia. In 1936 the *Discovery II* found 36 on Bird Island. Since then growth has been rapid, and now the population on Bird Island and neighbouring coasts is again hundreds of thousands. Helped by close protection in places under government control, and by the Antarctic Treaty and its Conventions farther south, they will continue to flourish in their old haunts. The

18

Elephant Seals, which seem to recover more readily than the Fur Seals, are also thriving, though they were taken under licence by the twentieth-century whalers.

Search for new hunting grounds in the early nineteenth century led to the discovery of new islands. Macquarie Island was discovered by Frederick Hasselborough, master of the *Perseverance*, while searching south of New Zealand, and named after the Governor of New South Wales. Sealers made many discoveries among the South Shetlands and neighbouring islands, though they tended to keep their findings to themselves; George Powell and Nathaniel Palmer found and charted the South Orkney group in 1821–22. Mr Charles Enderby, owner of the London whaling firm Enderby Brothers, and one of the founders of the Royal Geographical Society, took care to employ captains with more lively interest in exploration and charting than might be expected of most sealing captains. In 1806 one of his captains, Abraham Bristowe in the *Ocean*, discovered the Auckland Islands south of New Zealand. In 1808 Captain Lindsay of the Enderby whaler *Swan* sighted Bouvet Island and gave a more accurate position. The crews of two boats sent ashore there from the Enderby sealers *Sprightly* and *Lively* in 1825 remained weather-bound on shore for a week. Another Enderby man, John Biscoe, named Cape Ann, a prominent headland of Enderby Land, part of the continent, in 1831. In 1832 he sighted Adelaide Island and landed among the Biscoe Islands off the west coast of the Antarctic Peninsula, which he named Graham Land. John Balleny discovered the group that bears his name in 1839, and named each island after Enderby's partners in the voyage.

There were other captains of more than ordinary ability. In the course of his second voyage in 1821–22, George Powell made surveys resulting

Figure 5
Elephant Seal with pup, South Georgia,
17 October 1928

19

20

in the first reliable charts of the South Shetlands, the Bransfield Strait, and, with Nathaniel Palmer, of the South Orkneys. He made many soundings, studied the tides and currents, and recorded sea and air temperatures. Like Wales on Cook's second voyage, he found the water at 195 fathoms warmer than that at the surface, and, at least when his work was written up, knew of similar layering in the Arctic. Peter Kemp in the *Magnet* discovered Heard Island and Kemp Land the part of the continent east of Enderby Land in 1833.

James Weddell, who reached 74°15′ S in the Weddell Sea in 1823, wrote careful accounts of the coasts he visited, giving reliable positions, soundings, details of anchorages, observations of the winds and weather and made maps of the South Shetlands and the islands near Cape Horn. He reasoned well about the temperatures in relation to the altitude of the sun, commenting on the frigidity of latitudes which are temperate in the Northern Hemisphere. He made careful measurements of magnetic variation and knew about ship's magnetism. He showed an extensive knowledge of previous voyages and records. Condemning the wholesale slaughter of seals, he maintained that there should be some control: the mothers should not be killed till the young were ready to take to the water, and even then only older seals with a proportion of the males. It sounds very heartless now, but it was liberal then. He applauded the system practised in the island of Lobos on the north side of the entrance to the estuary of the River Plate, where the Governor of Monte Video was applying restrictions and closed seasons to prevent extermination. Lots of seals still go to Lobos.

The sealers made some mistakes: their Emerald, Dougherty and Nimrod islands do not exist.

Figure 6
Young Island, one of the Balleny Islands,
3 February 1936

21

Nineteenth-century explorers   Two Russian ships, the *Vostok* (East) and the *Mirnyi* (Peaceful), were sent by Alexander I on a voyage round the world under Captain Thaddeus von Bellingshausen in 1819–21, their main purpose being to supplement the work of Captain Cook. Hurriedly laid plans for the expedition received an early setback when two German naturalists, due to join in Copenhagen, failed to turn up, causing Bellingshausen to make what seems to be the only complaint in his long narrative, regretting that he had not been allowed to take two students of natural history from his own country. Even so his artist, Paul Mikhailov, produced many fine paintings and sketches. Bellingshausen must have been the first explorer to make regular use of a tow-net: a home-made net always hung at the stern of his ship. It caught more during the night than during the day, and he realized that the small drifting animals move up in the dark and down in the light. He made what seems to be the first clear reference to the small shrimp-like *Euphausia superba* which is the main food of the large southern baleen whales and many other animals; some penguins, carried aboard in a sack, threw up a great quantity of these shrimps which evidently formed their food.

Bellingshausen surveyed the south-west coast of South Georgia that Cook had seen from Cape Disappointment, leaving the names of some of his people on the map. He then surveyed the South Sandwich Islands, mapping and naming the ones Cook had not seen at the northern end of the group. Continuing south-east he saw through falling snow in 69°21′ S 2°14′ W a solid stretch of ice continuous from east to west. Although he thought he was looking at an ice field, he was probably looking at the ice cliffs that fringe the continent in that region. Farther east, in 69° S 16° E, he again saw ice cliffs and gently rising snow slopes beyond. After wintering in Australia and among the Pacific islands, he again sailed south-east and discovered Peter I Island, in what is now called the Bellingshausen Sea. A few days later he discovered Alexander I Land, now known to be an island. He then entered the Bransfield Strait, meeting American sealers, and made a running survey of the south side of the South Shetlands. This like his South Sandwich survey was long accepted as a model of accuracy. During much of his circumnavigation Bellingshausen was well south of Cook's tracks, restricting still farther the possible northern limits of the continent.

In early 1829 HMS *Chanticleer*, on a voyage to establish the figure of the earth by pendulum measurements, to make magnetic observations and to verify the longitudes of many places in the North and South Atlantic Oceans, sailed from Cape Horn to Deception Island. Her hydrographical, meteorological and magnetic observations were reported in an account of the voyage by W. H. B. Webster, the surgeon, after the tragic death of the captain, Henry Foster, in the River Chagres, on the way home. On the outward and return voyages across the Drake Passage, the directions of the currents were observed to vary widely, though mainly between north-east and south-east, and the speeds between 6 and 41 miles a day. Temperature measurements, made with a maximum and minimum thermometer, showed south of 60° S a surface temperature of 39 °F and a subsurface minimum of 34 °F; the relatively high surface temperature would prevent their maximum thermometer from recording a 36 °F in the warm deep water like that observed by Wales and Powell with direct reading instruments hauled up in insulating containers.

Notes were made on navigation in the South Shetland group, and on the island's geology and natural history. They did not see a single Fur Seal. Webster mentions that there were 'plenty of a small species of

24

shrimps, but they were not fit to be eaten'. The pendulum measurements, made in Pendulum Cove at Deception Island, lasted nearly two months, from 7 January to 4 March. There was abundant evidence of subterranean heat in many parts of the island, though the temperature of the sea was not affected; it varied between 32 and 37 °F, and during one night was entirely frozen over.

In 1829–31 Captain Edmund Fanning's expedition, supported by public subscription in the United States, visited the South Shetlands. James Eights, the naturalist, published a note on icebergs, and on the geology and natural history of the islands. He found a piece of fossil wood in the conglomerate below the basalt in Deception Island – the first fossil from the Antarctic. He described several of the small marine animals living on the shores or in shallow water.

Within the next few years there was growing scientific interest in Antarctic voyages. One of the fresh incentives was a convincing prediction, by the German physicist Carl Friedrich Gauss, that the south magnetic pole would be discovered in 66° S 146° E. Improvement of the magnetic charts was a major issue, and the newly formed British Association appealed to the government to sponsor an Antarctic expedition to the magnetic pole. At the same time United States citizens, led by Jeremiah N. Reynolds who had sailed with Fanning and Eights, were promoting further exploration, and in 1836 Congress authorized the United States Exploring Expedition. In Britain the Royal Geographical Society considered a pamphlet by its secretary, referring to the news that the USA was preparing to launch an expedition, and while urging the need of magnetic observations, still held out the possibility of discovering lucrative new sealing grounds. The British Association gave further support in 1837 and 1838.

Figure 7
The Antarctic coast in 69°58' S 1°31' E,
4 March 1939

25

The French government, knowing of these proposals, was the first to take action. The *Astrolabe* and *Zelée* sailed from Toulon early in 1838, under the command of Admiral Dumont d'Urville, who had served on a round-the-world voyage in 1822–25, and commanded another in 1826–29. On his new, Antarctic, voyage he named islands sometimes visited by sealers near the northern tip of the Antarctic Peninsula, but was disappointed in not being able to reach as far south as Weddell. After a year among the Pacific islands, he again turned south and, on 20 January 1840, discovered the continent in about 66° S between 136° E and 142° E. He landed on a rocky islet close to the shore, and collected rock specimens. He named the land Adélie Land in honour of his wife.

After his previous voyage, he had tabulated all the deep-sea temperature observations he could find, as well as his own, and concluded that in the open ocean the temperature at great depths was nearly constant, between 39 and 41 °F. He assumed that sea water, like fresh water, had its maximum density at about this temperature, and sank to fill the deep ocean basins. He concluded further that there must be a circumpolar belt somewhere between 40° S and 60° S where the sea, having this temperature at the surface, would have the same temperature all the way to the bottom. He thought that the surface water farther south continued to float at the surface because it was colder than the deep water, and the surface water farther north remained at the surface because it was warmer than the deep water. He ought to have known that sea water does not have a point of maximum density like fresh water, and continues to increase in density till it freezes, but like many hasty, plausible, assumptions the idea lasted a very long time in spite of abundant, clear, evidence to the contrary – it reappeared in Hansard on 12 April 1961. Charles Wilkes, commander of the United States Exploring Expedition, and James Clark Ross commander of the British Voyage to the Southern Seas, believed it, and their scientific advisers at home made the same mistake.

Two of Wilkes's five ships made a brief visit to the northern islands of the South Shetland group early in 1839, while the others tried to penetrate the ice in the Bellingshausen Sea. Early in 1840 he sailed south again towards the islands that Balleny had discovered a year earlier, and charted a series of landfalls and appearances of land between 160° E and 90° E in about 65° S. There was some confusion about what was part of the Balleny Islands, and what was continent. Ross later sailed over some of the appearances of land, and another Enderby captain, Tapsell in the *Brisk*, is reported to have sailed westwards from the Balleny Islands in 1850 in a higher latitude than Wilkes as far as 143° E without seeing land, but Wilkes's observations left little doubt that there was continuous land or ice cliffs not much farther south.

Wilkes left his naturalists in Australia, but his narrative describes the rich animal life seen in high latitudes, and refers on several occasions, to the multitudes of shrimps, concluding that it was these swarming animals that attracted the whales in such large numbers. He noted that they were also the food of the penguins. One of his midshipmen caught an Emperor Penguin, and he gives a graphic account of a Killer Whale attacking another whale. A description of the shrimps, based on a specimen collected, and sketch and colour notes, by one of the ship's officers, was published in 1855 by James D. Dana, one of the scientists left in Australia. It is the first comprehensive description of *Euphausia superba*, now so well known as 'krill', the principal food of the Antarctic whales, and the basis of a growing industry.

The expedition led by James Clark Ross in the ships HMS *Erebus* and

HMS *Terror* made comprehensive studies of the ocean as well as remarkable geographical discoveries, particularly of the deep embayment now known as the Ross Sea. He saw the mountainous coast of South Victoria Land, the active volcano of Mount Erebus, and the great ice barrier, no more penetrable than the cliffs of Dover. After wintering in Hobart, and visiting Port Jackson and New Zealand, he sailed to the eastern end of the ice barrier and survived a very stormy season south of the Pacific Ocean before spending the next winter in Tierra del Fuego and the Falkland Islands, where they hopefully planted 800 trees brought from Hermite Island. Early next summer they experienced the dangers of the Erebus and Terror Gulf in the north-west corner of the Weddell Sea. Farther east they reached 71°30′ S in 17°20′ W, between the earlier tracks of Weddell and Bellingshausen. Ross made another search for Bouvet Island, without apparently having seen the observations of the Enderby sealers, and arrived home in September 1843.

Failing, in the early part of his voyage, to gain soundings with 600 fathoms of line in the deep ocean, he made a line 3600 fathoms long, afterwards lengthened to 5000 fathoms, fitted with swivels to prevent its strands unlaying during descent, and strong enough to support a weight of 76 pounds. Since the ship could not be kept stationary in the water, and her drift would drag the line from the vertical, he mounted the big sounding reel in a boat kept head to wind by another. He logged the times taken by each successive 100 fathoms of line to run off the reel. They became longer as more line entered the water, partly because of some buoyancy in the line and more friction with the water, but there was usually an additional, obvious, slowing when the weight struck the bottom. In relatively shallow water the reel would almost stop, and when hauling in it was easy to feel the extra strain when the weight was lifted off the bottom. In very deep water, the slowing down was more difficult to recognize, especially if a current was pulling at the line. Using this method, Ross made sufficient deep soundings to give a clear indication that the circumpolar ocean was one in which abyssal depths separated the Antarctic continent from its northern neighbours. One of his soundings often quoted to demonstrate the difficulty of the method was his failure to find bottom at 4000 fathoms in the Weddell Sea, but a modern graph of the running out times that he logged shows a detectable slowing down at 2200 fathoms, now known to be about the right depth.

He made many deep temperature measurements with maximum and minimum thermometers, which, like the measurements collected by Dumont d'Urville, generally showed 39·5 °F below 600 fathoms, and he crossed the 'circle of uniform temperature', where the thermometers showed 39·5 °F at all depths, at six places round the circumpolar ocean between 50° S and 60° S, in much the same latitudes as we find the same surface temperature today. The true temperature near the bottom is only about 32 °F (0 °C), the differences from Ross's figures being due to the effect of pressure on the early thermometers. Ross remarked on the sharp fall in temperature, in both air and sea, as he approached the coast of South Africa near Saldanha Bay; he had expected warmer conditions as he neared the shelter of the land. Instead, he had to contend with a cold northward current that grew colder towards the land. He found that it was some 60 miles wide, and 200 fathoms deep, and marked by a cloud of mist over the cold water. Leaving Sydney in August 1841 he found a warm current.

Magnetic observations, one of the main objects of the voyage, were made assiduously at sea and at observatories erected on land and islands they visited, notably at Hobart and in the Falkland Islands. 'Term Days' when simultaneous observations were being made specially in other parts of the world had special attention. Ross was disappointed that the French and American ships had forestalled him in making observations between 140° E and 160° E, near the magnetic pole, but must have felt more than compensated by the remarkable geographical discoveries that followed his more easterly approach near 170° E.

While making his magnetic and pendulum observations at Hobart, he became interested in the studies of slow changes in mean sea level being made there, and decided to mark mean sea level in the places he visited, when he could stay long enough to make the necessary tidal records. In the Falkland Islands he deduced it from five month's tidal observations at Port Louis, and made permanent marks on a rock near the water's edge, and on the face of a nearby cliff; the Navy has recently rediscovered them, as well as the well-marked site of the magnetic observations. Five years later, while wintering in Port Leopold near the north magnetic pole, he studied the effect of varying atmospheric pressure on sea level, afterwards called the water barometer effect.

The two-volume account of his Antarctic voyage excites admiration of the breadth of his interest in subjects outside the usual versatility of a navigator, and readers are continually entertained by his accounts of things going on around him.

Ross was himself an accomplished zoologist and indefatigable collector, and his surgeons, Robert M'Cormick and John Robertson, and assistant surgeons, Joseph Dalton Hooker and David Lyall, were chosen for their interest in natural history as well as medical capabilities. They dredged the sea bed down to 400 fathoms, and used a deep-sea grab to collect samples from much greater depths. Ross noted that among the creatures he was taking, there were several that had been found when he was serving with his uncle, John Ross, in the Arctic. He maintained that the extreme pressure at great depths does not harm the animals that live there. Grabbing up shellfish with mud from 1000 fathoms, he predicted, contrary to scientific opinion at the time, that life goes on at all depths.

The greater part of the *Erebus* and *Terror* fish collection, originally very large, was lost or damaged beyond recognition, mainly because of overcrowding of specimens in spirit which, during the long period at sea, must have become too weak. However, Sir John Richardson, the naval surgeon and eminent icthyologist, who examined it was able to describe as many as 234 species, of which no fewer than 145 were new.

Wilkes also made a very large collection of fishes along the icy barrier off Wilkes Land, off the South Shetland Islands and off the southern coasts of South America, Australia and New Zealand. It would have been largely the basis of our present knowledge if it had received the attention it deserved. Wilkes estimated that the description would need 2000 printed pages, but Louis Agassiz of Harvard College, to whom it was entrusted, was never able to complete the work; presumably the necessary funds and assistance could not be obtained. The manuscript seems to have been lost, and many of the fishes and labels too. It was not till 1923 and 1940 that careful reports dealt with what remained.

Much of Ross's zoological collection suffered an even worse fate. John Murray in the historical introduction to his *Summary of Results* of the *Challenger* expedition, 1873–76, writes that although Ross was an indefatigable collector it is to be regretted that the large collection of deep-sea animals, which he retained in his own possession after the return of the expedition, was found to be totally destroyed at the time of his death. Had they been carefully described during the expedition or on its return to England, the gain to science would have been immense, for not only would many new species and genera have been discovered, but the facts would have been recorded in journals usually consulted by zoologists, instead of being lost sight of as was the case. Murray tells us that a large number of drawings made by Hooker during the voyage were handed to the specialists working on the *Challenger* material, and they showed that some of the *Challenger* discoveries had been anticipated by Ross.

Anyone who has had anything to do with expeditions knows that it is more difficult to raise funds for detailed study and publication of the results than for the work at sea. We can feel the deepest sympathy with Ross, who, after the hardships of his Antarctic voyage, another winter in the Arctic in the search for his Hobart friend Sir John Franklin, the loss of his wife, and while caring for his children, could not do justice to a large zoological collection. It needed fighters like Wyville Thomson and John Murray, able to devote their whole energy to the business, able eventually to get the funds, and able to secure assistance from a wide range of specialists to do a similar, though undoubtedly greater, task with the *Challenger* collections.

There were some highlights in the natural history. Joseph Dalton Hooker, who joined the expedition at the age of 21, was a great help to Ross and lived to help twentieth-century explorers. He wrote extensively about the phytoplankton, that was so abundant as to discolour the water and stain the ice. His *Flora Antarctica*, published in 1858, laid the foundations of the botany of the Antarctic ocean and islands. He recognized the importance of winds and currents in establishing distribution patterns. Another important contribution was made by Christian Gottfried Ehrenberg who studied microflora in the water, ice and sediment samples sent to him. Robert M'Cormick's report on the geological results was published in two large volumes in 1884.

Richardson related a curious incident which occurred when the ships were far south in the Ross Sea. In strong winds a fish was blown from the sea and frozen in the ice round the bow of HMS *Terror*. When chipped out it was taken to Robertson; he made a sketch, but before he could preserve it the ship's cat sneaked into his cabin and ate it. The sketch was not sufficient for identification, but Richardson reproduced it in his report under the name *Pagetodes* meaning frozen stiff. Many years later, Professor Dollo, of Brussels, reporting on the fishes collected by the *Belgica* expedition, 1897–99, suggested that the strangely come-by sketch should be identified with his *Cryodraco antarcticus*, of which the Belgian expedition obtained one specimen. He reproduced Robertson's sketch, noting, among other details, 'Mangé par le chat de l'équipage de la Terror'.

Ross's expedition brought much new information about the circumpolar ocean and its coasts and islands, particularly Kerguelen, South Victoria Land, the Ross ice barrier, Auckland and Campbell Islands, the coasts of Tierra del Fuego, the Falkland Islands and the Erebus and Terror Gulf. Although very successful during his first season among the ice in 1840–41, the two following seasons showed how difficult and dangerous the Antarctic ocean can be. One of his most remarkable achievements was the health record in his ships: after each long, trying, cruise into the icy seas, they returned to port without a single name on the sick list.

In 1845 Lieutenant T. E. L. Moore, afterwards governor of the

Falkland Islands, sailed south from Simons Town in the chartered ship *Pagoda*, manned by volunteers from the South Africa station, to fill in magnetic details south of the Indian Ocean. They encountered much bad weather, and a surprising number of icebergs, but could claim to have seen more of the ocean south of 60° S than previous explorers in this region. He reported a mass of rock, that appeared to be a rocky islet in 60°42′ S 4°03′ E but ships searching for it find only deep water. The *Pagoda* was the last ship to go to the Antarctic without auxiliary power.

HMS *Challenger* sailed from Simons Town in December 1873 and, after visiting Prince Edward, Marion, Kerguelen and Heard Islands, crossed 60° S on 10 February 1874. She saw her first iceberg in 61° S, reached her farthest south (66°40′ S 78°22′ E) on 16 February, and crossed 60° S again on her way to Australia on 28 February. During what was a very brief cruise her powerful new methods, and the thoroughness with which all her work was done, led to many scientific discoveries. Dredging in the iceberg region produced rocks similar to those found on other continents though not occurring on oceanic islands. They obtained information about the water layering, though with some difficulty because their maximum and minimum thermometers though protected against pressure registered only the highest and lowest temperatures encountered. The biological studies were the foundation of much future work.

The report on ocean circulation by Alexander Buchan, the Scottish meteorologist, based on the *Challenger* results and other observations, remarked on the need for a broad southward movement of salt water to balance the effect of all the cooling and dilution that goes on in the Antarctic, but does not identify it with the warm layer found by Cook and Powell. He produced the first overall picture of the distribution of atmospheric pressure over the Antarctic ocean, finding a circumpolar ring of low pressure some 30 degrees wide, in which the mean pressure falls to about 29 inches of mercury (980 mb) in 63° S, beyond which 'as shown by the prevailing winds' it begins to rise into higher latitudes.

There was another circumnavigation, by the German corvette *Gazelle*, in 1874–76. She visited Kerguelen, but afterwards remained in low latitudes till finally crossing the eastern half of the Pacific Ocean in 47–52° S.

Nineteenth-century whalers

As soon as the new coasts and harbours on the borders of the circumpolar ocean were discovered, the Sperm Whale, the chief object of pursuit during the American whaling period in the eighteenth century, was followed there; although living mainly in tropical waters it migrates towards temperate waters in summer, and some of the males, probably those not able to command a mating herd, go to feed in high latitudes. The coasts of Peru and Chile were found very profitable, and by 1802 activity had spread to New Zealand, and then to the Indian Ocean. Sperm whaling reached its peak in 1837, though the number of ships engaged rose to 824 by 1842, 594 being American. The Southern Right Whale was pursued at the same time; its name came from the North Atlantic and implied that it was the right whale to catch, because it was slow, frequented coastal waters and floated when killed, and could therefore be taken by hand harpoons and boats putting out from the shore. It ranged from 15° S to 60° S, but was most abundant between 30° S and 50° S, and enormous numbers were taken by whalers working from coasts, islands and ships, mainly between these latitudes. Sir Sidney Harmer, lecturing to the Linnean Society on the history of whaling said that 193 522 were taken between 1804 and 1817. Professor Dakin gives a graphic account of 'Bay' and 'Deep-sea' whaling in his *Whalemen Adventurers*. After 1840 the Right Whale fishery steadily declined due to overfishing. Small numbers appeared among the large catches of Blue and Fin Whales in the early twentieth century, and they were given complete protection by international agreement in 1937.

Humpback Whales, though more agile than Right Whales, were fairly easily approached and often taken, but they were not so vulnerable as Right Whales, and did not suffer as much depredation till steam whaling and the ship-mounted harpoon took over. The early whalers would often fill up with oil from Elephant Seals, whose decline was not as complete as that of the Fur Seals, possibly because relatively small returns for much labour made the hunting less thorough, and because the Elephant Seals recuperate more quickly after reduction in numbers.

Svend Foyn developed his harpoon gun in 1868 at the time when the Northern Right Whale grounds had successively been worked out and were almost deserted. It revolutionized whaling by enabling the capture of the more powerful Blue and Fin Whales. Boats were no longer needed: the whale was shot directly from the bow of the ship, and the heavy harpoon and its line were strong enough to hold the whale and raise it to the surface. The use of accumulator springs to take the strain of sudden jerks off the line was an important part of the development. It was some time before the new methods were generally adopted, but new whaling stations were set up in Norway, the Shetlands, Hebrides, Faroes and Iceland, and it was then not long before they could be seen to be having an adverse effect on all species of whales in the North Atlantic. Sigurd Risting in his history of whaling published in 1922 wrote that it was declining in every respect and seemed fated to come to an end in a few years time. Norway banned whaling from her own coastal waters in 1903 because it seemed to be harming the fisheries, restoring it only much later when seeking concessions elsewhere.

It was under these circumstances that the whalers turned to the south, to the reports by Weddell and Ross of large numbers of whales in the Weddell Sea. The first reconnaissance was made from Hamburg and Bremen, by Captain Eduard Dallmann in the steam whaler *Grönland* in 1873–74. She made discoveries off the west coast of the Antarctic Peninsula, found American sealers at work in the South Shetlands, and reported seeing large numbers of whales, but not Southern Right Whales. In 1892–93 four whalers were sent from Dundee to the Weddell Sea, and one, the *Jason* commanded by Carl Anton Larsen, the pioneer of Antarctic whaling, was sent from Norway. William S. Bruce, who afterwards led his own expedition, went with the Dundee whalers but found little time for science. They had guns that would fire harpoons slightly farther than men could throw them, but still had to work from boats. The whales they saw were the fast-swimming kind, mostly Blue and Fin, and although they put three harpoons in a Fin Whale and managed to pass all three lines to one of the ships, the whale broke them all. They got as much oil as they could, by very laborious hunting of Crab-eater Seals that haul out on the ice; they saw no Fur Seals and few Elephant Seals. Larsen was less discouraged than the Dundee whalers and sailed again in 1893; this voyage was most remarkable in that he was able to sail as far as 68°10′ S down the east coast of the Antarctic Peninsula. At the same time two more Norwegian whalers, the *Hertha* and *Castor*, were exploring the west coast; they obtained full cargoes of seal oil, but saw no Right Whales.

Another Norwegian whaler, the *Antarctic*, financed by Svend Foyn, sailed south from Australia in 1894. She forced her way through the pack ice and sighted Cape Adare, the northern end of South Victoria Land, on 16 January 1895, the first time it had been seen since Ross discovered it 54 years earlier. The voyage was not a commercial success; they saw no Right Whales so far south, and could not take the more powerful whales. It was not till 1904 that ships competent to catch them began work in the Antarctic, at South Georgia.

Late-nineteenth-century explorers

There were three mainly scientific expeditions in the late nineteenth century, in the *Belgica*, 1897–99, the *Valdivia*, 1898–99, and the *Southern Cross*, 1898–1900. The *Belgica* visited the South Shetland group and made discoveries among the islands farther south. She was beset in the Bellingshausen Sea ice, south of Peter I Island, for 12 months in 1898–99 – the first expedition to winter in the Antarctic, though 11 sealers from the *Lord Melville* had survived the winter of 1821 on King George I., and all but one of an American sealing gang had died there in the winter of 1877. The *Belgica* had a comprehensive scientific programme. A rich collection of fishes and bottom-living animals was obtained by dredging and trawling widely on the continental shelf. Using modern deep-sea reversing thermometers, they made measurements down to 4000 m compatible with those we make today. In their summer observations in the southern half of the Drake Passage the surface temperature was above 0 °C, but decreased to −1 °C at about 100 m, before rising above 2 °C in the warm deep layer and falling again below 1 °C in the cold bottom water. The temperatures throughout the water column decreased towards the south, and on the continental shelf most of the water column had a temperature near the freezing point of sea water, not far from −2 °C, especially in winter. Only very close to the bottom, where, in this region, some of the warm deep water creeps on to the shelf, did the temperature rise above 0 °C.

July was the coldest month and February the warmest. The drift of the ship, and the ice in which she was locked, was found to depend mainly on the wind, with some indication of an additional cyclonic circulation, westwards near the continental slope and northwards east of Peter I Island. Emile Racovitza, the expedition's zoologist, made careful observations of whales, becoming acquainted with the different species, and combining his own evidence and earlier reports to make studies of their distributions and factors likely to affect them. He referred to the great abundance of krill far south in the Bellingshausen Sea, noting the heavy toll exacted on it by penguins and Crab-eater Seals, and stating that krill appeared to be the food of the Humpback Whales. F. A. Cook, the ship's surgeon, whose attempt, later on, to reach the North Pole caused such a stir, and who more than pulled his weight during the *Belgica* voyage, remarked on the full meal of shrimps obtained by Adélie Penguins from narrow leads in the solid pack far south in the Bellingshausen Sea. The *Belgica*'s physical, biological, geological and meteorological observations, geographical discoveries and charts, were published in detail in ten large volumes, in a fine style like those of French expeditions and the *Challenger* Reports.

The German Deep-Sea Expedition in the *Valdivia*, a former Hamburg–America liner, carrying ten scientists with modern equipment, made a brief visit to Antarctic waters as part of a much wider study of the Atlantic and Indian Oceans. Leaving Cape Town on 13 November 1898 she found Bouvet Island, fixing its position accurately for the first time,

comparing it with those previously reported, and questioning the existence of Thompson Island reported by George Norris, a sealing captain, in 1825. Excellent photographs showed a small island, 5 to 6 miles across, almost completely ice capped. A remarkable sunset painting, by F. Winter, the expedition's artist, is reproduced in colour in the account of the voyage by its scientific leader Carl Chun, first published in 1900. They made 30 deep soundings with wire sounding machines, taking bottom samples, most of them deeper than 500 m, between Cape Town, Bouvet, Enderby Land, Kerguelen and St Paul Island. They had wire ropes for hauling shallow and deep nets and bottom trawls. The Antarctic surface water had a rich phytoplankton and zooplankton, and there was a rich bottom fauna at depths between 400 m and 600 m round Bouvet Island. A successful bottom trawl at 4636 m in 63°17′ S 57°51′ E brought up a great load of continental rocks, granite, gneiss and schist, and a huge block of sandstone weighing a quarter of a ton. The *Valdivia* reached to within 100 miles of Enderby Land before being turned back by the ice.

Two vertical series of temperature measurements showed the typical three-layer structure, Antarctic surface water, warm deep water and cold bottom water. Their salinity values, deduced from density measurements, were not very consistent but showed the low salinity of the surface water, the high salinity of the warm deep water, and a slight decrease into the cold bottom water. Professor G. Schott, beginning his career as a world authority on the geography of the oceans, remarked on the particularly low temperatures near Bouvet Island, believing it to be directly influenced by a polar current, now identifiable as the Weddell Sea current that carries cold water and ice across the Atlantic sector. Most of the expedition's reports were published within ten years of its

Figure 8
Bouvet Island, showing Kaiser Wilhelm Peak bearing S 59° W distant 6·8 miles, 18 October 1930

return, but were still appearing as late as 1932. They also contain many remarkable photographs.

The *Southern Cross* expedition of 1898–1900, financed by the publisher Sir George Newnes, was more adventurous and less sophisticated. It was led by Carsten Egeberg Borchgrevink who had been on the Norwegian whaling reconnaissance to the northern edge of the Ross Sea in the *Antarctic* in 1894–95. They intended to make coastal surveys, botanical, zoological and mineralogical collections, meteorological, magnetic and pendulum observations, and to reach the magnetic and south poles. The expedition could not really hope to achieve all this, but its shore party was the first to winter on the continent, at Cape Adare from which egress to the interior proved too difficult. Next year parties from the ship made short sledge journeys on the Ross ice barrier. The zoological results were described by well-known scientists in a volume published by the British Museum (Natural History) in 1902, though the collections had suffered in transit, and notes made by the enthusiastic and capable Nicolai Hanson, who died at Cape Adare, had been lost. The rock specimens were described by Sir Archibald Geikie, and the magnetic and meteorological observations by Louis Bernacchi, physicist on the expedition, and, soon after, on Scott's first expedition.

Early-twentieth-century scientific exploration

Between 1900 and 1914 fourteen ships carried expeditions to the Antarctic continent, and although science, particularly at sea, was subservient to exploration and polar journeys, much was learnt about the science as well as the navigation and hardships of the ocean. Except for a few deep-sea temperatures and soundings, the oceanography of Scott's first expedition was limited to the rather remarkable work of

42

Thomas V. Hodgson, the biologist, near the *Discovery*'s winter quarters in McMurdo Sound. Although his net hauls, made in a relatively small area, tended to be repetitive, they produced rich collections which were worked on by many specialists after the expedition returned. He obtained the first specimens of *Euphausia crystallorophias*, sometimes mistaken for *Euphausia superba*, but found mainly very close to the coast of Antarctica. It swarms there and is probably eaten largely by whales, seals and penguins near the head of the Ross Sea.

Hodgson also made the interesting discovery that between June and October ice crystals soon formed on the lines he used to haul his nets under the ice from one hole to another. Within 48 hours the ice crystals would mainly coat lines between depths of 9 and 15 m, though on a line left for three days in the coldest month, they went down to 30 m, and the line, 0·6 cm in diameter, was coated to a diameter of 30 cm with ice crystals. A line left below 20 m was not usually coated. We now know that the freezing point of sea water, generally about $-1·9\,°C$, is lowered by pressure below the surface, and that underlying water near an ice shelf can be cooled below the surface freezing point without freezing, but if it is stirred upwards, possibly by wind or tidal forces, ice crystals will separate, especially if there is a nucleus for them to form on. They were a nuisance to Hodgson, and damaged his specimens. The expedition's reports were published between 1907 and 1918, the biological and geological results by the Natural History Museum, and the physical results, including the work on tides, by the Royal Society. On the way home across the Pacific sector the *Discovery* made deep soundings and found deep water round the reported position of Dougherty Island.

The German South Polar Expedition of 1901 was predominantly

43

scientific. It was financed by the government. Under its leader, Erich von Drygalski, it made extensive observations and collections in the Atlantic and south-west Indian Oceans, as well as in the Antarctic. After visiting the Crozets, Kerguelen and Heard Islands, they sighted the continent in 90° E, but their ship, the *Gauss*, was trapped and frozen in the ice some 50 miles short of it. While locked in the ice, they showed that the water on the continental shelf was almost uniform, close to freezing point in winter and only slightly warmed at the surface in summer. Current measurements made through a hole in the ice showed that the current was mainly directed by the east wind, with some deflection to the south due to the effect of the earth's rotation. Occasionally there were northward deflections, which were expected because of the north-west trend of the coastline and the presence of a projecting ice shelf a little farther west. The direction of the current did not change with depth, being roughly parallel to the coast and moving at about 8 km a day. They found the transition zone between predominantly east and west winds in about 60° S, and north of this the current was mainly towards the east.

One of the most widely significant findings was the recognition by the expedition's meteorologist Wilhelm Meinardus that the West Wind Drift has a natural division into two parts, a southern cold-water region, directly influenced by Antarctic freezing and melting, and a northern mixed-water region in which the temperature rises more rapidly towards the north. The transition zone between them, where the cold water slips below and mixes with the warmer water, is marked by a relatively sharp change of surface temperature. Meinardus plotted its course between 105° W and 80° E, from all the data available, and it was afterwards called the Meinardus line, and later the Polar Front or Antarctic convergence.

Special attention was paid to the deep and bottom layers. The temperature of the warm deep water was shown to decrease towards the south as it mixed with the colder overlying and underlying waters, and to fall below 0° C near the outer edge of the continental shelf. The bottom water was judged to be a mixture of shelf water and deep water, and in drawing this conclusion Drygalski, whose report was not published till 1927, had also the evidence obtained by Professor Wilhelm Brennecke on the next German Antarctic Expedition of 1911–12. North of the Meinardus line they traced the low salinity of the Antarctic surface water, sinking below 1000 m into an Antarctic intermediate layer, like that which Brennecke found spreading northwards in the Atlantic Ocean. They had been measuring the oxygen, nitrate, ammonia and carbon-dioxide contents of the water, for correlation with studies of phytoplankton growth, and found the Antarctic intermediate layer to have a high nitrate content like that of the Antarctic surface water, and much higher than that of surface water in lower latitudes where the plant nutrients get used up.

Discussing the southward bend of the ice edge between 60° E and 80° E noted by all ships traversing the region, Drygalski believed that it was not due to southward flow at the surface, though it might be associated with strengthened southward flow in the warm deep layer.

While still in the ice, sledge journeys were made to the neighbouring land, where there was a prominent mountain which they named Gaussberg. They studied tides and tidal streams, measuring the rise and fall of the ship with the help of a wire anchored to the bottom by a weight. They also measured the internal temperature of icebergs, finding that below 15 m their temperature was nearly constant at −10 °C.

The main emphasis of the biological reports was on the taxonomy and details of occurrence of the different species, but they also contain information on distribution in relation to the water movements, and also on the general seasonal migration, upwards in the summer and downwards in winter. Emil Philippi, the expedition's geologist, made a notable study of the stratification of the deep-sea sediments, finding diatom ooze, typical of the Antarctic zone, below globigerina ooze, typical of warmer water, suggesting a retreat in Antarctic influence since an earlier ice age.

The Swedish South Polar Expedition, 1901–03, led by Otto Nordenskjöld, sailed in the *Antarctic*, the whaler that went to the Ross Sea in 1894, and now captained by C. A. Larsen, who commanded the *Jason* in the Weddell Sea in 1892–93 and 1893–94. After examining the west coast of the Antarctic Peninsula as far as 65° S, they tried the east side but were turned back by ice just before the Antarctic Circle. Nordenskjöld and his wintering party landed to make their base on Snow Hill Island in the Erebus and Terror Gulf, near Seymour Island where Larsen had made the first well known find of Antarctic fossils in 1893. After landing Nordenskjöld, the *Antarctic* went north to the Falklands and South Georgia. At the beginning of the following season she worked in the Bransfield Strait, but was then crushed in the ice of the Erebus and Terror Gulf on her way to Snow Hill. All her crew managed to get ashore on the nearby Paulet Island, and eventually they and the wintering party were rescued by the Argentine ship *Uruguay*.

The Swedish soundings added to knowledge of the submarine arc that runs from Cape Horn through the Burdwood Bank to South Georgia and the South Sandwich Islands and doubles back through the South Orkneys to the Antarctic Peninsula and the South Shetlands. This is now known as the Scotia Arc, bending round the Scotia Sea. The *Antarctic* made temperature and salinity sections between the Falkland Islands and South Georgia, across the Bransfield Strait and eastwards from the Antarctic Peninsula in 66–64° S. This would have been a particularly valuable section if the sampling above the continental slope had been reliable below 400 m. It is a very inaccessible region, and only very recently has T. D. Foster, working from an American icebreaker, been able to secure sufficient observations to show the shelf water sinking down the continental slope to form Antarctic bottom water.

The expedition's biological studies were fully reported, one volume of the reports appearing as late as 1960. The remarkable fossil collection from Snow Hill, Seymour Island and nearby sites, showed that they once had a much warmer climate, possibly like that of southern Chile.

The Scottish National Antarctic Expedition, 1902–04, led by William S. Bruce, in the *Scotia*, sounded, trawled and dredged extensively in the Weddell Sea, making large contributions to the natural history of the seals, birds and penguins, and rich collections of the fishes, plankton, marine sediments and algae. They discovered Coats Land, the south-eastern coast of the Weddell Sea, a continuous ice cliff with no rock outcrops. The expedition wintered in Scotia Bay in the South Orkneys, studying the botany, geology and glaciology, and setting up a meteorological station, which, after the voyage, was taken over by the Argentine meteorological service. Bruce was not able to find money for more than six volumes to present the expedition's results, but they were published extensively in well-known scientific journals. The temperature and density measurements were not discussed in detail, but Brennecke made good use of them in 1918, when he showed that the deep water is warmer near the southern margin of the Weddell Sea than it is farther north, being part of a westward movement from the Indian Ocean sector that circles clockwise round the Weddell Sea, and comes out of what Professor Schott called the ice cellar of the Atlantic very much modified. It accounts for Captain Cook finding open water south of 60° S in the south-west Indian Ocean, while he still had an eastward pointing tongue of ice to the north of him.

Two French expeditions, in the *Français*, 1903–05, and *Pourquoi Pas?*, 1907–10, both led by Jean-Baptiste Charcot, carried out programmes of charting, geology, glaciology and botany, and of meteorological, magnetic and tidal observations, but measured little at sea, only surface temperatures and a few shallow vertical series. Shackleton's 1907–09 expedition which reached to within 97 miles of the south pole, as well as getting to the magnetic pole and climbing Mount Erebus, did some dredging in McMurdo Sound. John King Davis, in charge of the *Nimrod* on the way home, helped to disprove the Royal Company Islands, named after the Spanish Royal Company, and also Emerald and Dougherty Islands.

The *Terra Nova* used by Scott on his second expedition, dredged and trawled in the Ross Sea. Edward W. Nelson the shore party's biologist made a long series of very precise temperature measurements through a hole in the ice near the winter quarters, and his water samples, analysed long after the expedition's return to England, mostly gave reliable values for salinity. Too little interest was taken in his work, but when it was finally assembled and published in 1975, in the *Polar Record*, it could be seen that he had anticipated the much later discovery of a striking increase of salinity in the Ross Sea due to salt being left behind when sea water freezes. Like Hodgson he found ice crystals forming on his line, though not till August; he was 12 miles farther north than Hodgson, and farther from the ice shelf. The crystals began to form when the water had cooled without interruption to the freezing point corresponding to its salinity, and ceased to form just before the temperature showed any perceptible increase.

Nelson fished plankton nets through holes in the ice, the current usually being strong enough to stream them out. Tidal observations showed that only one tide a day was perceptible when the moon was far north or south of the equator; when it was near the equator there were two, more or less equal, but small tides. When the ship used a bottom trawl in McMurdo Sound it was common to find half the animals dead. They commented on the large size that some species attained there in comparison with that of related species in warmer waters, except for the ones that required calcium for their skeletons. They found enormous siliceous sponges. In the Ross Sea undecomposed phytoplankton was found 4 inches below the surface of the bottom mud, presumably preserved by the low temperature.

Denis G. Lillie, the ship's biologist, went northwards with the ship to New Zealand during the winter, making collections on the outward and return voyages, and writing an account of whaling in New Zealand waters. As with Scott's previous expedition, the biological results were published by the Natural History Museum. Those of the mainly shore-based geological, glaciological and magnetic studies, were published with the help of the Captain Scott Memorial Fund, raised by public subscription.

The *Fram*, that had carried Amundsen to the Bay of Whales, used the winter of 1911 in the South Atlantic Ocean, making two oceanographic sections from South America to Africa, with temperature and salinity measurements, mostly down to 1000 m, at stations 100 miles apart. The work was attractively reported by Bjorn Helland-Hansen and Fridtjof Nansen in an appendix to *The South Pole*, published in 1912, but it does not say anything about the Antarctic ocean. During her visit to Buenos Aires, the *Fram* was lying close to the *Deutschland* which was taking the second German South Polar Expedition, led by Wilhelm Filchner, to the Weddell Sea.

The *Deutschland* carried the outstanding oceanographer Dr Wilhelm Brennecke, who had already studied the Atlantic, Indian and Pacific Oceans on a round the world voyage of the research ship *Planet*. In the *Deutschland* he had modern equipment, including both protected and unprotected, reversing deep-sea thermometers. The thermometers are attached to a water sampler that is clamped to a thin wire rope; the wire is paid out till the sampler reaches the depth from which the measurements are required and then a small streamlined weight is clipped round the wire and let go. Reaching the sampler, it strikes a lever which triggers the device, enclosing the water sample and reversing the thermometers. Reversal separates part of the mercury thread in the thermometers. In the one that is protected from the pressure of the surrounding water the separated thread is a measure of the temperature at the depth of reversal, needing only a small correction for expansion of the small separated amount of mercury when it is read off inside the ship. The unprotected thermometer separates a longer mercury thread because of the effect of pressure as well as temperature, and the difference between the two readings, after suitable calibration, gives a good measure of the depth of sampling, generally more accurate than the length of wire paid out because ship's drift, and sometimes currents, drag the wire away from the vertical.

Brennecke also had the recently developed method of determining salinity by titrating the chloride content of the sample, and the application of such positive techniques over a long stretch of ocean brought immediate results. A preliminary report sent home from Buenos Aires on the way south showed that a relatively warm and highly saline deep current flows southwards from the north Atlantic at depths between 2000 and 3000 m, below a less saline, and sometimes colder intermediate layer with its nucleus at 600 to 800 m. The new figures helped in the interpretation of the *Gauss* observations, and in reappraisal of those of the *Challenger*, *Gazelle* and *Valdivia* which led to rather sharp correspondence between the two outstanding, but apparently rival, laboratories at Hamburg and Berlin, about the relative achievements of the earlier workers. It became clear that much more could have been made of the *Challenger* observations if they had been given the same thorough study as the biological collections; the temperature measurements were generally left to the ship's officers.

Filchner was not able to set up a base on the Antarctic continent, but Brennecke made temperature, salinity and oxygen measurements as far south as 77°40′ S on the continental shelf in the Weddell Sea. He continued his careful measurements as the ship, locked in the ice, drifted to the north, first through a well, opened up when the propeller was raised, and later, when ice pushed under the ship, through a hole in the ice. His full report, published in 1921, left little doubt that Antarctic bottom water is formed by mixing of the deep water, already considerably cooled during its clockwise circulation into the southern part of the Weddell Sea, with water cooled and raised to a high salinity

51

by freezing on the continental shelf. He made measurements of the alkalinity and pH of the water, and compared the carbon-dioxide content of the water with that of the overlying air, finding the water of the Weddell Sea richer than the atmosphere, as can be expected if the surface water is mixed to some extent with deep water, especially at times when there is little photosynthesis. He studied the small salt content of ice formed from sea water, and its decrease with time, especially where the ice is raised above the surface. There was a close relationship between the wind and the drift of the ice and ship which moved at 2·78 per cent of the wind speed, and at an angle of 30 degrees to the left of the wind. Professor H. Lohmann, their expert on oceanic plankton, only went as far as Buenos Aires, but even so made useful progress in relating plankton species to water conditions.

The next German expedition, the German Atlantic Expedition in the *Meteor*, was even better prepared. Studies by Alfred Merz and Georg Wüst, and by Schott and Brennecke, of the circulation of water in a vertical section along the Atlantic Ocean had provided fresh stimulus and new ideas, and the *Meteor* was amply staffed and fully equipped. She made a remarkable survey of the temperature, salinity and oxygen at all depths in the South Atlantic Ocean, describing surface, subsurface, intermediate, deep and bottom layers in great detail and linking them with Antarctic water types during an extended cruise in the Atlantic sector of the circumpolar ocean.

Discussing the cold bottom water Wüst agreed with Brennecke that it is formed by water sinking from the continental shelf mixing with deep water, but thought that some part must be played by surface cooling on a wider scale. Although the warm deep water had never been found exposed and subject to direct cooling at the surface, he thought that in winter there might be some centres of downward stirring strong enough to upset this usual stable layering. This conclusion was supported by finding, as Brennecke had done, that the deep water in the northern part of the Weddell Sea is colder than that farther south, though it now seems more likely that the low temperatures are due to cold water flowing eastwards after circulating all round the Weddell Sea. There are, however, two exceptional areas where almost complete vertical mixing, from surface to bottom, has been observed; one of them, known for a long time, is between the South Shetland Islands and the South Orkneys in a boundary region between the current flowing out of the Weddell Sea and that coming through the Drake Passage. Another, recently discovered by Arnold Gordon, is close to the transition between east and west winds and near some irregular bottom topography, in 67° S 7° W.

The *Meteor*, being the first ship to use an echo sounder on such a large scale, and taking a sounding every 20 minutes, produced more detailed bathymetric charts. In the circumpolar ocean she produced a clearer picture of the submarine ridge joining the South American Andes with the Antarctic Peninsula, then known as the South Antillean Arc, and discovered the South Sandwich Deep outside the convex chain of islands, the deepest sounding being 8050 m. Farther north the results showed how the Walvis Ridge, joining the Mid-Atlantic Ridge to Africa, could effectively hold back the Antarctic bottom water from the east Atlantic basin.

The *Meteor* biological studies were largely confined to studies of plankton taken in surface nets and micro-organisms from water samples. She made extensive studies of the chemistry of sea water. Some measurements of the gold content, made for Fritz Haber, gave rise to the story that there was some hope of using it to pay war debts, but, for any purpose, the amounts were too small for economic recovery. There were also surveys of alkalinity, pH and carbon dioxide, and measurements of phosphate as a guide to the availability of plant nutrients. Measurements of the currents were made at ten deep anchor stations, and meteorological observations, including upper-air measurements were made continuously throughout the voyage. Some 30 deep-sea bottom cores were taken during the Antarctic cruise, including 28 cm of grey-green ooze from 6772 m in the South Sandwich Deep.

The success achieved in this outstanding study of the deep circulation and mixing processes did much to increase interest in exchanges between the Antarctic and warmer waters.

Growth in the study of the circumpolar ocean had not been so rapid on the other side of the world, but John King Davis, taking Douglas Mawson and the Australian Antarctic Expedition of 1911–14 to their bases on Macquarie Island and the continent, made many soundings, trawls and dredgings. The collections, together with those from the shore bases and their botanical, geological, glaciological, meteorological and magnetic observations, were published in a series of reports which, like those of most of the earlier expeditions took 25 years to write.

Shackleton's 1914–16 expedition sailed in the *Endurance*. He had tried to buy the *Björn*, which soon became the *Deutschland*, but found her too expensive. His ship became locked in the ice before a land base could be established, and drifted north 200–300 miles west of the previous track of the *Deutschland*. Shackleton's party made a unique line of soundings, and collected information on the winds and currents; like Drygalski and Brennecke, they found that the drift of the ice depended mainly on the wind. Not many of the biological results seem to have survived, but we can read that the stomachs of the 1436 Gentoo Penguins used to feed the stranded men on Elephant Island were full of *Euphausia*, probably *E. superba*, which seems to show that they are plentiful in winter. Shackleton's last expedition in the *Quest* made useful contributions to the natural history of South Georgia, Elephant Island, Gough Island and Tristan da Cunha. A collection of papers describing the geological results was published by the Natural History Museum in 1930.

Twentieth-century whaling

Antarctic whaling was started by C. A. Larsen, who had captained the *Jason* in 1893–94, and the *Antarctic*, for the Swedish South Polar Expedition in 1901–03. After landing Otto Nordenskjöld, leader of the expedition, on Snow Hill Island, Larsen took the ship to the Falkland Islands and South Georgia. As well as visiting Jason harbour in West Cumberland Bay, where he had anchored the *Jason* on his previous voyage, and Moltke harbour, where German scientists had maintained a station during the first International Polar Year in 1882, he anchored for a month in Grytviken, which meaning 'pot harbour' was named from the old iron pots left there by sealers: one of the pots is now outside the Scott Polar Research Institute in Cambridge, England. In 1903, after the *Antarctic* had been crushed by the ice and they had been rescued by the Argentine ship *Uruguay*, he was able to promote Argentine interest in whaling, and the Compania Argentina de Pesca was formed. Returning to Norway, he fitted out an expedition of two sailing ships and a steam whaler, which arrived in Grytviken in December 1904. They built a station and started work without the knowledge of the Falkland Islands government which soon stepped in to regulate the industry, setting a limit to the number of stations and catchers that could operate in the Falkland Dependencies, prohibiting the killing of any whale calf or female accompanied by young, and requiring that all the whale should be used with as little waste as possible.

In the early days the carcases had been set adrift after only the blubber had been stripped, and the beaches round about are still jumbled with their bones. The early factory ships, like that which began whaling in the South Shetlands in 1905–06, at Deception Island, were particularly wasteful; the whale was flensed in the water and the pieces of blubber hauled on board, the most difficult being left. Less than half the amount of oil later obtainable from the meat and bones as well as the blubber was recovered.

The number of whales caught in the Falkland Dependencies each year rose to 12 000 by 1911–12, but the proportion of Humpback Whales in the catch was declining sharply, leaving no doubt that too many were being killed. The catch was changing to the more difficult Blue and Fin Whales, and the catchers were having to go much farther from their stations to find whales. It was then that the industry, taking such toll, began to accept the need and afford facilities for study of the reproductive habits, growth rates, migrations and physiology of the whales, and for scientific exploration of the ocean.

In 1910 Jens Andreas Mørch, a Norwegian whaling engineer, made a direct approach to the Natural History Museum in London asking that every vessel catching whales under British licence should record the place, species and sex of every whale caught, whether the females were pregnant, and relevant environmental data. Dr Sidney F. Harmer, Keeper of Zoology at the museum since 1909, and in charge of a large collection of whale material, communicated a paper by Mørch, urging closer study of the Antarctic whaling grounds, to the Zoological Society of London in 1911. He also persuaded the museum trustees to make representations to the government about the serious threat to the whales, showing how all the earlier whaling grounds in the Northern Hemisphere had been denuded one by one, and now the same tragedy was being enacted in the Antarctic. An inter-departmental committee on whaling and the protection of whales was set up in 1913, to take evidence from whaling managers and scientists, and one of the museum's specialists, Major G. E. H. Barrett-Hamilton, was sent to South Georgia to gain first-hand information. The committee had to suspend its meetings during the war, but published its evidence in 1915, and was followed by another interdepartmental committee, on Research and Development in the Dependencies of the Falkland Islands, in 1917. This led to the Discovery Investigations in 1924, which soon showed how the falling size and age composition of the catches could be monitored, and provided more and more evidence that too many were being killed.

The changes at South Georgia were continuing: Humpbacks, once particularly prized for the large size of their whalebone, or baleen – the large filtering plates that retain the krill scooped into the whale jaws – had almost disappeared from the catches, and a smaller whale not previously hunted much, the Sei Whale, was being taken in greater numbers. The most striking change was the development of factory ships that could operate on the high seas independently of shore stations. The older factories had needed a sheltered anchorage so that they could flense the whale in the water alongside the ship, and a plentiful supply of fresh water for their cookers. The new factories were large enough to haul the whales up on deck through a slipway in the

57

stern, to carry all the plant and equipment to make full use of the blubber, meat and bones, and to turn most of the refuse into guano fertilizer. They could carry enough fuel oil for themselves and an increasing number of catchers, and as the fuel and stores were used up, their tanks and stowage were used for the oil, meal and guano they produced. They also were serviced by transports coming to them in mid season. C. A. Larsen who pioneered the whaling at South Georgia, again pioneered the new development with a 13 000 ton vessel, the *Sir James Clark Ross*, in the Ross Sea in 1923–24. Much larger ships were used later on, averaging about 20 000 tons; they had the great advantage of mobility, being able to follow the whales without having to be near land. They generally worked near the edge of the pack ice, where the whales tended to congregate, where the winds were usually not so strong, and where they could usually get some shelter inside marginal ice streams.

By 1930–31 the annual catch at South Georgia had fallen to 8000, but the total Antarctic catch had risen to 40 000. This was too much for the market, and there was much reduced activity in the following season, but although there were increasing signs of overfishing, half the catch being immature whales, the number killed rose to 46 000 in 1937–38. After falling to a low level during the war it was 31 000 in 1953–54, and averaged 33 000 a year between 1957 and 1962. By then it included an increasing number of Sei Whales, and the proportion of the more profitable Blue Whales was rapidly diminishing. The paradoxical situation had emerged in which whaling was growing in inverse proportion to the whale stocks: the daily production of factory ships sank to less than half its former amount although they were using an increasing number of catchers – up to 15 – and a Soviet factory used 18 and finally 24. Rapid decline followed, and it took only a few years to complete the destruction. There was no whaling in South Georgia in 1962–63, and after two of the stations had been leased to Japanese whalers for a short period in 1963, whaling closed down there entirely. By 1968–69 the annual catch of Antarctic baleen whales had fallen below 1000, and in 1972 the UN Conference on the Human Environment called for a ten-year ban on whaling.

Britain and Norway had long insisted on compulsory regulation of their whalers, the manager of an expedition being responsible for seeing that only the number of whales that could be fully worked up were killed, protecting whales of each species shorter than specified minimum lengths and keeping detailed records. Whaling Inspectors were carried to see that all the rules were obeyed as far as possible.

There had also been attempts at international regulation, beginning in 1937 and 1938 with conferences that set minimum lengths to protect the younger, immature whales of each species, giving total protection to Right Whales, temporary protection to Humpbacks, setting opening and closing dates to shorten the hunting season, and establishing a sanctuary in the Pacific sector in which no whales could be taken. In 1944 an overall limit to the annual catch was agreed, but it was set in Blue Whale units, according to a scale in which 1 Blue = 2 Fin = $2\frac{1}{2}$ Humpbacks = 6 Sei. This, instead of fixing a quota for each species as the scientists wanted, led to selective depredation of the more profitable species one after the other, Blue being the first to go.

A new international regulating body, the International Whaling Commission, was set up in 1946. It meets annually but has generally been submissive to commercial and national interests, having only limited powers to make regulations and no power to enforce them. In the midst of a welter of formal, practical and political objections, and

59

60

inevitable finding of loopholes in any convention, it was not till 1972 that separate quotas for each species were agreed on. By then it was too late: the stock of whales had been reduced to something like a tenth of its former size, and by 1980, except for one Japanese and two Soviet factories catching Minke Whales, Antarctic whaling came to an end. The Minke Whale was named after a gunner named Meincke who made himself a figure of fun by killing such a small animal in mistake for a Blue Whale.

Throughout the sorry story whalers contended that the reduction in numbers would not lead to extermination. They argued that, in contrast to the North Atlantic, where, at least in the early days, a whaler could show some profit if he caught only one whale, to send a factory to the Antarctic costs a million pounds, so that the whales would be left alone before they were reduced to levels from which they could not recover. There begin to be some indications that protection is leading to small increases in numbers, and, helped by new revulsion of public feeling to the slaughter of whales, the Whaling Commission is likely to be strong enough to prevent further fishery in which the rate of catching exceeds the rate of replacement. There is little doubt that if a reasonable quota of 10 000 or so could have been established in 1937–38, when the threat to the industry was so clearly apparent, such an annual catch could still be supplying the world with some 200 000 tons of oil and 300 000 tons of meat. It must, however, be recognized that the main motive of the industry in its later years was profit rather than a real world need for whale oil, amply filled by vegetable oils, and only the Japanese really needed the meat. Something like $1\frac{1}{2}$ million whales were taken from the Antarctic ocean.

Figure 9
Deception Island and abandoned whaling station, 3 March 1932

62

The Discovery Investigations

The expansion of the whaling industry and threat to the whales emphasized the need for more information about their reproductive habits, growth rates and migrations, and about factors that might vary their numbers and distribution. The British government appointed the Discovery Committee to plan the necessary work, with Sir Sidney Harmer, by then Director of the Natural History Museum, as Vice-Chairman. The work was financed from a research and development fund built up from a tax on whale oil processed in the Falkland Dependencies, which was increased to 5 shillings a barrel in 1919, though, because the whaling companies were already meeting difficulties, no more than $3\frac{1}{2}$ shillings was ever charged. The companies were given a written assurance that the money would be devoted to research in the Dependencies, mainly with the view of preserving the whaling industry. In spite of some resentment at the tax the companies did much to help the scientific studies, providing facilities, especially opportunities to work on the whales they were processing, without which the research could not have been done.

The scientists set up a laboratory close to the whaling station at Grytviken, and, from 1925 to 1931, carefully examined some 3700 whales, looking particularly for evidence leading to better understanding of breeding, growth, age, food, and the range of variation of dimensions and external characteristics. Most of the whales undertook long migrations, northwards in winter to breed, and southwards in summer to feed, so the whale studies were extended to the whaling stations at Saldanha Bay and Durban, on the west and east coasts of South Africa, during the winter months. Scientists were also sent in factory ships, and, in all, some 6000 whales were closely examined. One of the most immediate tasks was to develop methods that would allow

Figure 10
The whaling station at Grytviken, South Georgia, summer 1925

64

the records of species, sex and length, made by the whalers, to be used for monitoring the age and maturity of the whales that were being killed.

The early studies showed that recognizable traces of past ovulations were retained in the ovaries of the females, the number varying from none in the youngest to more than 50 in whales that were obviously very much older, some additional indication of age being obtained from the number of scars on the body surface, and, particularly of physical maturity by the rigidity of linkage of the vertebrae. There was also a method, fairly reliable for young baleen whales, based on counting small ridges on the baleen plates attributable to annual variations in the rate of formation of new material near the growing point. A later method counted laminations in a long, conical, horny plug present in the whale's ear, which helps to transmit sound to the middle ear. There was some uncertainty whether there were one or two laminations a year, but accumulating evidence from the return of marks fired into the blubber many years earlier eventually showed one a year. This method proved the most serviceable being applicable to both sexes and all ages. Sperm Whale ages were determined from laminations in their teeth. Blue and Fin Whales were sexually mature at two years old, and already 74–78 and 64–66 feet long; they become physically mature a few years later.

Studies of whale migrations were made by marking them with numbered darts fired from a shoulder gun, and comparing the place and date of marking with details available after the whale was captured. By 1975 the number marked by *Discovery* scientists, and later in an international scheme, was 8234, of which 10·5 per cent were recovered. A further 1224 were marked and 11 per cent recovered by a Soviet

Figure 11
The whaling station at Grytviken, South Georgia, winter 1925

scheme. They confirmed the earlier conclusion about the main north and south migrations, especially for the Humpbacks, which follow the coasts and get taken by the whalers working in coastal regions. There is rather little information for Blue Whales, which seem to be more dispersed in the warmer water, and whose numbers were declining by the time marking became fully effective.

The longest interval between marking and recovery ranged from 11 years for a Sei Whale to 37 years for a Fin; further interpretation is difficult because of the decline of the industry and the protection of some species. Marks found in whales studied in detail by biologists, or from which specimens were obtained, gave useful checks on the methods of age determination, and it seems that the big Antarctic whales, if not hunted, may live as long as 80 years.

It was apparent from the start that detailed knowledge of the ocean would be necessary for assessment of the factors likely to lead to natural variations in abundance and distribution of whales, such as those that might influence reproduction and food supplies. The purpose of the northward migration in winter is to seek warmer water for breeding, though there is little to eat there and they depend on the fat stored in their blubber and other tissues. In summer the southward migration, and subsequent Antarctic distribution, seems to depend on that of their food supplies, mainly the swarming *Euphausia superba* (krill), and on the ice that allows or prevents access to their principal areas of abundance. The distribution of the krill appears to depend on water movements that favour their reproductive cycle and transport of the early larval stages to other areas.

The Discovery Committee, set up in 1923, was an impressive group of men who had achieved eminence in related interests, but without

Figure 12
Male Blue Whale, 79 feet long, on the flensing platform at Grytviken, 12 March 1927

anyone with up-to-date experience in deep-sea oceanography. They bought the *Discovery*, used by Captain Scott on his first expedition, before appointing the scientific director and his staff, who might have recognized that a speedy, widespread, network of observations across the ocean was beyond the capability of a square-rigged sailing ship. They also built a smaller, fully-powered steamship the *William Scoresby*, named after the master whaler, for whale marking and trawling, as well as oceanographic surveying. The work of the two ships is described very attractively by Sir Alister Hardy in his *Great Waters* but there was something of a crisis in the Committee's affairs when, after the first voyage, the very able scientific director, Dr Stanley Kemp, had to insist that the *Discovery* must be replaced by another fully-powered steamship.

The *Discovery II* was all that could be desired. The building contract was signed with Ferguson Brothers on the Clyde in February 1929, and she was at work in the Antarctic in January 1930. Her total cost including scientific winches and engine-room spares was only £67 000. She made five 20-month voyages to the Antarctic before the war, and another afterwards. She had a tough time during the war, being among the first ships off the Normandy beaches, laying buoys. After the war she served the National Institute of Oceanography and many university scientists till 1962, when she could no longer hold the growing numbers and equipment needed for modern science.

In the Antarctic, the whole of the circumpolar ocean was fairly well covered with routine temperature measurements and water sampling from the surface to the bottom, and with vertical, oblique and horizontal net hauls, down to 1000 to 1500 m. It was sufficient to give a good idea of the distribution patterns of plankton and whales in relation to the more easily plotted physical and chemical patterns, and

Figure 13
The Royal Research Ship *William Scoresby* leaving Grytviken, South Georgia, for work in the Humboldt current, 10 April 1931

eventually to useful correlations with the winds, currents and other water movements. Although many of the conclusions were perhaps oversimplified, they are still usable.

It took a long time for the Discovery scientists to distinguish and become familiar with all the 18 stages in the life history of *Euphausia superba*, the principal food of the whales. However, the still greater task was that of going through all the samples, covering the whole horizontal and vertical range of distribution, and, as far as possible, at all times of the year, sorting, counting and measuring the different stages in the life history of *Euphausia superba* and other important species and studying them in relation to what was known of the temperature and current patterns. There are other difficulties in interpreting the figures due to the varying capabilities of different species and different stages of their life histories for avoiding nets; the catches of near-surface nets are likely to be less in daylight for this reason as well as because of the general downward migration of many species in daylight.

The Discovery Investigations continued for 25 years, and it is remarkable that the average cost, over the 10 years after the *Discovery II* was at work and before the war, was only £48 250 per annum, including all the cost of work at sea and at home. Even so there was always a threat, especially as receipts from the tax began to fade, that each voyage would be the last, and experienced scientists, knowing how long such work takes, began to leave for more stable positions so that new ideas were not passed on as effectively as they might have been, and some of the value of hard-won experience was lost. In 1949 the work was handed on to the newly-formed National Institute of Oceanography, afterwards the Institute of Oceanographic Sciences.

Thirty-seven volumes of the *Discovery Reports* have been published.

Figure 14
The Royal Research Ship *Discovery II* in Port Lockroy, 21 January 1931

Figure 15
HMS *Ajax* joining the search for a survey party
missing from RRS *Discovery II* off the north
coast of King George Island, South Shetlands,
18 January 1937

They contain systematic accounts of the phytoplankton and zooplankton, as well as of the whales and other mammals, and much information on their distributions, particularly of the krill. Much more could be done with the collections, based on some 20 000 net hauls, carefully preserved and documented, but such long-term study is not easily financed, nor is it very suitable work for young scientists without much prospect of following up their findings in the Antarctic ocean itself. Perhaps growing interest in the ocean as well as the continent will lead to further use of what is unique material. Work today has to be concentrated in logistically accessible areas, near or on the way to land bases, and on problems that lead to almost immediate publication; covering the ocean as a whole at the critical times of the year to solve long-term distributional problems has become too expensive.

The old *Discovery* was used by the British, Australian and New Zealand Antarctic Expedition led by Sir Douglas Mawson in 1929–31, making physical, biological and other scientific studies along the continental margin south of Australia and the Indian Ocean.

Widening scientific exploration

From 1927 to 1931 observations by the *Norvegia* near Bouvet Island, South Georgia, Enderby Land, and finally all round the circumpolar ocean, allowed Hakon Mosby to add much to our knowledge of the different water types and their movements. Further important contributions were made by Johan Hjort and J. T. Ruud from the whaling factory *Vikingen* in 1929–30 along the Weddell Sea current between the South Orkneys and Bouvet Island, particularly on the development and growth of the larval stages of krill. Observations were made from the *Sir James Clark Ross* in the Ross Sea in 1928–29, and from the *Thorshaven* between 1932 and 1937. The *Brategg*, financed by the Norwegian Whaling Federation, made useful observations in the eastern Pacific sector in 1947–48. The *Jan Wellem*, the first German whaling factory, was used to study the Weddell Sea current across the Atlantic sector, finding evidence of its variability and tendency to move as a series of eddies. In 1939 the *Schwabenland*, taking flying boats to look at the continent, made a series of physical observations along the Greenwich meridian.

There was rapid expansion in exploration after the war, though much of it seemed largely concerned with the land and territorial claims. Argentina, Chile and Britain established bases on the Antarctic Peninsula and neighbouring islands, but apart from observations on seals, penguins and birds, their marine studies were limited. The USA also became active. A relatively large expedition to the Antarctic Peninsula and the Ross Sea in 1939–41 was followed by a wider study, south of the Pacific and Indian Oceans in 1946–47. It used 12 ships, aircraft and a submarine. The coastal lands were plotted from the air, and landing parties made extensive geological and glaciological studies. At sea they made extensive use of the Bathythermograph, an instrument much used during the war to obtain temperature profiles from the surface down to a depth of 250 m without stopping the ship.

Closely spaced vertically continuous profiles showed the temperature structure to be much more complex than it appeared from the earlier widely spaced sampling at discrete depth intervals, and called attention to 'internal waves', of tidal and shorter periods, in density layering below the surface. Using more powerful echo-sounders than were available before the war, the American expedition members saw 'deep scattering layers', echoes from plankton and fish, migrating upwards at sunset and downwards at sunrise. They added much to our knowledge of the topography of the sea floor and, with improved bottom corers, learnt much that was new about the sediments. Except for studies of seals, birds and penguins, the biological studies were mainly of the phytoplankton, taken from water samples. Since the expedition had 4000 men it seems rather a pity that more effort could not be devoted to marine studies.

From 1949 to 1952 a joint Norwegian, British and Swedish expedition occupied a base at Maudheim, near the coast in 4° W. The scientific studies were mainly in meteorology, including the upper atmosphere, glaciology and geology, including seismic sounding, but Harald U. Sverdrup, visiting the base in 1952, measured sea temperatures, salinities and currents. The French Polar Expedition maintained a base on the coast of Adélie Land between 1950 and 1953; the work was mainly on land, but they also studied the coastal birds, animals and plankton. They made careful studies of the tides, of long-period waves caused by atmospheric depressions passing between the continent and Australia, and of microseismic activity caused by sea waves. The Australian National Antarctic Expedition, which had maintained bases on Macquarie and Heard Islands in 1947–48, established its Mawson station, south of Kerguelen, in 1954, and kept it active during the International Geophysical Year.

Study of the ocean was a rather secondary objective in the Antarctic IGY programme, but many observations were made, especially by ships from the USA and Soviet Union, the American ships working mainly in and near the Ross Sea, and the Soviet ships south of the Indian Ocean. More information was obtained about the bottom topography. As noted in earlier studies, ships approaching the continent found their

75

soundings sloping up to about 300 m at the edge of the continental shelf and then sinking again to 500–1000 m, sometimes to as much as 2000 m, before rising slowly again to the land. The outer banks are believed to be moraines, formed when the continental ice shelves extended much farther north. An alternative hypothesis, not so favourably supported, is that the depressions are cracks formed when the continent was sinking under its great weight of ice. South of the Indian Ocean the IGY scientists found many extinct submarine volcanoes, with fragments and streaks of volcanic rock piercing the sediments.

The water sampling brought more detailed maps of the physical and chemical properties, and information on the characteristics and structure of the water masses. The Soviet ships studied wave heights, finding that the maximum heights in storm areas exceeded 15 m, and sometimes reached 25–30 m. They gained new information on the distributions of pack ice and icebergs. Current measurements showed close dependence on the local winds. The biological studies south of the Indian Ocean showed that the zooplankton was richest between 50° S and 55° S, near the Antarctic convergence, and that in summer it was concentrated between 0 and 100 m. Bottom-living animals were most abundant near the Antarctic coast, their numbers decreasing rapidly with increasing depth and distance from the coast. Despite the low temperatures near the coast the phytoplankton was found to be abundant.

The US naval operation 'Deep-Freeze' overlapped and extended well beyond the IGY. Icebreakers and other vessels made extensive contributions to the oceanography of the Ross Sea sector, and scientists based at McMurdo Sound learnt much about the physics and biology of the inshore waters. One of the outstanding achievements of the icebreakers was the discovery of the Thurston Peninsula, now known to be a group of islands, that extends to 72° S between 96° W and 102° W, near to where Captain Cook reached 71°10′ S. One of the remarkable things about this coastal region was the paucity of bottom-living animals, contrasting with the usual richness of Antarctic coastal waters, and possibly due to the almost permanent heavy ice cover. From this time onwards USA activity increased, to culminate in the extensive research cruises of the *Eltanin* and *Hero* and many other researches and surveys financed by the National Science Foundation.

The USNS Eltanin   Built in 1957 as an Arctic-going cargo ship for the US Navy, the *Eltanin* was converted to a research vessel by the National Science Foundation in 1961, and then worked for $10\frac{1}{2}$ years in the circumpolar ocean. She was at sea 75 per cent of the time, making 55 cruises, each of two months, and only once returning to a port in the United States. She carried up to 39 scientists and a technical support party, and her crew were seamen from the Military Sealift Command, similar to the UK Royal Fleet Auxiliary. She served as a national research facility, made available to institutions able to undertake research in the Antarctic ocean with the help of the National Science Foundation. Unlike the *Discovery II*, which concentrated on the task of relating the plant and animal life histories and distributions to the water conditions, the *Eltanin* ranged widely over every aspect of marine science, some of the projects being immediate enquiries into problems that small teams working for two months every now and then might expect to solve.

The *Eltanin* oceanographical surveys were in contrast very long term

and continuous, making a momentous and lasting contribution to the basic study of the circumpolar ocean. The new *Southern Ocean Atlas*, mapping the temperature, salinity, oxygen content and plant nutrients, at all depths, published by the Columbia University Press, could not have been made without them. In 1972 the programme was discontinued for lack of funds, though the ship was operated for a time jointly by the USA and Argentina, and much was done to fill the gap she had left in the western Indian and eastern Atlantic sectors. She was handed back to the US Navy in 1979, but everyone hopes that she or a replacement will return to the Antarctic ocean. Taking full advantage of precision echo sounding and new techniques for seismic sounding, coring and bottom photography, she made great advances in the study of the ocean floor.

The physical and chemical observations showed that cold shelf water from the Ross Sea, and particularly from the shelf of Adélie Land, makes recognizable additions to the flow of bottom water from the Weddell Sea. The new data provide a much more complete network for studying the circumpolar current; although its surface speed generally averages less than half a knot, it is so wide and deep that it carries about 130 million metric tons of water a second, more than twice as much as the Gulf Stream. The close spacing and continuity of the new recordings, which replace the older sampling at positions rather far apart and at discrete depth intervals, emphasize the variability of the water movements, their horizontal patchiness, and the vertical interleaving of cold and warm strata, especially in transition regions.

The new geophysical techniques, including towed magnetometers and measurements of heat flow through the earth's crust, helped to develop the theory of ocean spreading, with new ocean floor formed by

Figure 16
Anvers Island across the Neumayer Channel from Port Lockroy, showing Mt Francais (9285 feet), 22 January 1931

material rising in rifts in the mid-ocean ridges, and that of 'plate tectonics', with moving sections of the earth's crust. Not surprisingly, the older maps of submarine ridges and ocean basins have been found to be oversimplified, the ridges being irregular as might be expected if they are formed by intermittent rising of new material, and interrupted every now and then by 'fracture zones' where they have been dislocated by lateral movements.

Successive levels in the bottom cores were dated by comparing their directions of magnetic polarity with sequences established from wider research, including the use of micro-organisms as age indicators. They have provided useful evidence in studies of changes in water conditions, ice cover and climate. Manganese nodules, with varying amounts of nickel and cobalt, were found, and the fracture zones suggested as likely sources of manganese. Bottom photographs showing scouring and build-up near irregularities were used to assess the direction and speed of water movements.

Although much of the *Eltanin*'s biology was done by teams using the ship for one or two cruises, findings in one sector are a good guide to what happens in the others. The phytoplankton studies showed rather striking differences between the open ocean, where the catches were often rather poor, and coastal and near-ice regions, where they were generally rich. The studies of fish included work on the physiology and biochemistry of icefishes that have no blood haemoglobin and increase their resistance to freezing by having large molecules and stabilizing substances, in solution.

The *Hero*, a small research vessel operated by the National Science Foundation in coastal waters on the west side of the Antarctic Peninsula and both sides of South America, has pursued a continuous biological programme since 1968. She has given much help to the US scientists at Palmer station, on Anvers Island, in their krill studies. Other US research vessels, *Atlantis II*, *Conrad*, *Knorr* and *Melville*, have studied wider areas. US icebreakers, whose main task is to open the way to the large base at McMurdo Sound as early as possible each year, have sometimes made unique contributions. The *Northwind* filled a big gap outside the north-east corner of the Ross Sea, where warm deep water reaches the continental slope with a temperature of nearly 2 °C. There have been many fruitful cooperative projects operated by the USA, such as the Fluid Dynamics Research and Kinetic Experiment (F-Drake), concerned mainly with the Drake Passage, the International Southern Ocean Studies (ISOS) studying the region south of New Zealand as well as the Drake Passage, and the International Weddell Sea Oceanographic Expeditions (IWSOE) that have built up our understanding of the currents and water masses of the Weddell Sea. Another project, Geochemical Ocean Sections Studies (GEOSECS), using the most accurate methods and advanced techniques in very detailed studies of the chemistry of the oceans, made observations south of the Atlantic and Indian Oceans, and south of New Zealand. Instead of trying to list all their contributions, it seems better to re-orientate towards overall pictures of what we know.

The winds and surface currents

Daily weather maps of the circumpolar ocean show four or five depressions spaced round it as in Figure 17. They travel mainly eastwards on varying tracks between slower moving high pressure areas farther north and a predominantly high pressure region over the continent. A ship standing in the path of the northern part of one of the

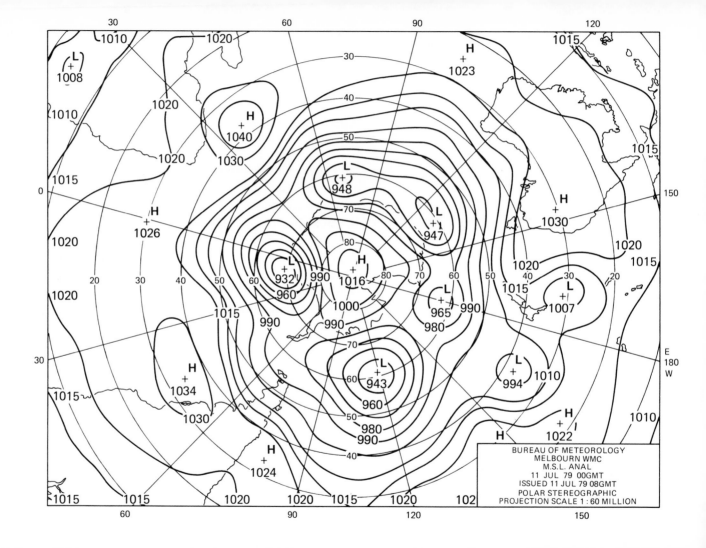

82

depressions experiences north-west wind, with heavy cloud and rain or snow as the barometer falls, followed by clearer skies and lower temperatures as the wind backs to the south-west and the barometer rises. These changes take place about twice a week as the depressions move eastwards at 20–25 knots. Standing in the path of the southern part of the depression the ship will find north-east wind and probably snow as the barometer falls, and clearer, colder weather as the wind veers to the south-east and the barometer rises. Although the depressions last a long time, they are not likely to travel all round the circumpolar ocean, some fill up, and new ones form, and the general trend is south of east.

Charts showing mean atmospheric pressure, averaged over a year, season or even only a month, show a much smoother picture, with a trough of low mean pressure in 60–65° S, between extensive subtropical regions of high pressure, in about 35° S in summer and 30° S in winter, and a large area of high pressure over the Antarctic continent. This leads to predominantly west winds, varying between north-west and south-west, north of 60° S, and to predominantly east winds, varying between north-east and south-east, south of 60° S. Such limits are only approximate and vary from one passing depression to the next so that there is a relatively wide transition region with variable and generally weaker winds. This is what Captain Cook found near 60° S in the Indian Ocean. In the Pacific sector the transition is 5 degrees or so farther south. The mean monthly speed of the west winds between 40° S and 60° S ranges from 15 to 24 knots; the east winds near the continent are generally much weaker. However, these are only average figures; everywhere there can be violent storms from time to time, and near the continent some remarkable calms.

Figure 17
Circumpolar weather chart for 11 July 1979
by the Bureau of Meteorology, Melbourne,
based largely on data transmitted from drifting
buoys (redrawn and slightly simplified)

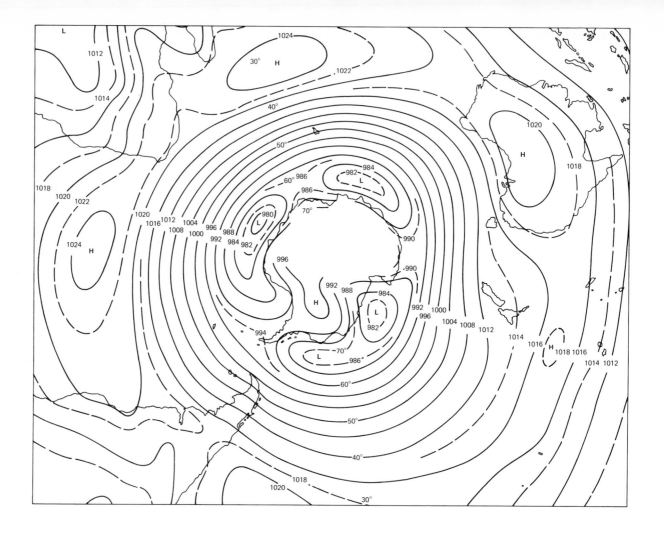

84

The winds and surface currents

The narratives of Antarctic voyages often refer to a westward current near the continent, commonly called the East Wind Drift, but we are not sure whether it is a continuous flow of water along every bit of the coast, or whether it is fragmentary, and composed of the southern segments of a number of clockwise circulations (gyres) in the boundary region between the east and west winds. Paul Tchernia and his colleagues of the Laboratoire d'Océanographie Physique persuaded Antarctic ships to mount his small satellite-monitored transmitters on icebergs close to the continent. Those that were not grounded or trapped in coastal basins travelled westwards at an average of 4 to 8 miles a day, with a maximum of 29 miles a day and occasional small backward loops to the east. Icebergs reaching the Ross Sea, the Balleny Islands, the southern end of the Kerguelen plateau and the Weddell Sea seem inevitably to turn northwards and make a U-turn into the West Wind Drift. This seems to support the idea of large-scale gyres, possibly linked to topographical features, and of fairly short segments of coast with weaker or more variable movements. One of Tchernia's recent results shows an iceberg wandering about for six months at an average of 4·3 miles a day without going more than 60 miles from a central point on the continental slope in 64° E, and then suddenly taking off for 1600 nautical miles along the continental slope to the west at 11·7 miles a day. Although the iceberg tracking shows much variation from time to time and place to place, vertical sections showing temperature and salinity distributions at right angles to the coast always show the density surfaces sloping downwards towards the continental slope, which is a reliable indication of westward flow.

The combined effect of the earth's rotation and friction on a wind drift is to produce water transport to the left of the wind in the Southern

Figure 18
Mean atmospheric pressure at sea level in July by the National Center for Atmospheric Research, Boulder, Colorado, based on all the available July observations of ships and land stations (redrawn)

Hemisphere. It is generally known as Ekman transport after V. W. Ekman, who worked out the theory to explain Nansen's observation, in the Northern Hemisphere, that the ice drifted to the right of the wind. Southward Ekman transport in the Antarctic East Wind Drift is one reason for the downward slope of the density surfaces. Another is the 'geostrophic effect' in which the effect of the earth's rotation on any water movement is to make the density layers slope downwards, to the left in the Southern Hemisphere, and to the right in the Northern Hemisphere. The angle of the slope is determined by a balance between the effect of the earth's rotation, which depends on the speed of the current and the latitude, and that of gravity, which depends on how far the density layers are tilted from the horizontal. Both factors may help to explain why ice remaining unmelted at the end of summer tends to hug the Antarctic coast, though in some places winds blowing down from the continent tend to drive it offshore.

Farther north the current flows mainly to the east, with some Ekman transport to the north. James Clark Ross sailing eastwards from Kerguelen, found his ship's position every day to be 12 to 15 miles ahead of his reckoning, convincing him that in these latitudes west winds blow almost as steadily as the Trade Winds and cause an eastward flowing current. Later on, south-east of New Zealand, he was carried south of east at 15 miles a day. Recent observations show that the current is mainly eastwards south of 40° S as far as 60° S north of the Weddell Sea, 63–65° S in the Indian sector, and 65–72° S in the Pacific sector. The average speed seems to be rather less than half a knot, though we know little about the day to day variations, and 1 to 2 knots has been reported.

Several drift bottles put out by W. S. Bruce were found many years later on the coasts of Australia and New Zealand, though it seems that they remained undiscovered in the sand too long to show the rate of drift. Others, which must have been spotted immediately, have indicated drifts of 12 to 18 miles a day. The Horace Lamb Centre for Oceanographical Research put out several thousand plastic drift cards south of Africa and the Indian Ocean, and recoveries from Australia, Macquarie Island, New Zealand and South America suggest drifts of 6 to 10 miles a day. A similar programme conducted by the Sea Fisheries Branch in South Africa led to 150 recoveries from islands south of the Indian Ocean, Australia and New Zealand indicating drifts of 5 to 7 miles a day. An enormous natural experiment happened when millions of tons of pumice were liberated by a submarine eruption 35 miles north-west of Zavodovski Island in the South Sandwich group, on 5 March 1962. On 14 March HMS *Protector* reported 2000 square miles covered with pumice, with large pieces floating on the surface and fine particles as deep as could be seen, enough to block the ship's condenser intakes. It began to reach Macquarie Island, Stewart Island and Tasmania in late 1963 and early 1964 and spread to all coasts of New Zealand during 1964. The reports mentioned large blocks, as well as marble and pea-sized granules. The largest pieces, sailing with the wind, travelled at about 16 miles a day, while the smaller particles, more likely to follow the water movement, averaged 6 to 9 miles a day. There were also later arrivals that might have been refloated after going ashore, or might have travelled by less direct routes.

Between October 1978 and December 1979 a large number of drifting buoys were put out in the circumpolar ocean to make temperature and atmospheric pressure observations and to transmit them several times a day to a satellite passing overhead. The system allowed the track of each buoy to be followed very closely. Although some of the buoys had drogues to anchor them to the water, we are not quite sure about the relative influences of wind and water on the drift, but the average drift, over meandering tracks between 40° S and 60° S, was 13 miles a day. Something rather less than half a knot seems a fairly reliable figure.

Although the West Wind Drift, now commonly called the Antarctic circumpolar current, must be driven primarily by the wind, its exact course must also depend on other factors. A number of instances have been shown of the effect of the topography of the sea floor, and likely mechanisms suggested. The current is deflected to the north in the middle of the Pacific sector by the mid-ocean ridge, and lined up along the mid-ocean ridge south of Australia. The direction of the current is commonly inferred from what has been called the dynamic topography, based on the slope of the density layers in the current, down to the left in the Southern Hemisphere. Owing to this slope, with the lighter water going to the left, the sea surface and other surfaces of equal pressure are higher on the left of the current. By calculating the densities from the temperatures and salinities at all depths such heights can be calculated, and if they are referenced to a pressure surface that is assumed to be level, which involves the assumption that there is no current there, the topography of the surface can be inferred, and one gets a map of the currents. Its contours, called dynamic isobars, indicate direction of flow like the isobars on a weather chart, and their distance apart gives a measure of the rate of flow, as those on weather charts show the wind strength. It works quite well in the warmer parts of the ocean where the water is well stratified, but probably not so well in the Antarctic ocean, where there must be a lot of mixing across the density surfaces and where, although the current decreases with depth, there is growing evidence that it is still fairly fast and variable at the bottom. Nor does the method take full account of wind stress or changing conditions, and we begin to see that the circumpolar current, like all the others, has varying bands of strong and weak flow.

During the past 20 years we have been able to measure currents by mooring a number of vertical series of internally recording current meters and leaving them for up to a year or more. The meters are clamped to a wire that is held vertical by some subsurface floats at the top, and weights sufficient to anchor it at the bottom. It is better not to have the supporting floats at the surface where they can be seen from ships and battered by waves; it is safer to operate a release near the anchor by coded acoustic signals from the ship and allow the supporting floats to come to the surface only when the meters are to be recovered. In the Antarctic it is sometimes risky to attempt measurements at depths less than 400 m above which the subsurface floats are likely to be fouled by icebergs; the loss of several moorings is attributed to such hazards.

US scientists have made such measurements over many years in the Drake Passage. They have also measured the vertical distributions of temperature and salinity, with observations sufficiently closely spaced to show the multiple core structure of the current. Even before this the old method of water sampling had been expedited by having as many as 15 samplers at intervals on the wire that lowered them to predetermined depths. When the first was closed and its thermometers reversed by a 'messenger' sliding down the wire, it released a second messenger for the second sampler, and so on till they were all closed. Occasionally there were regrettable incidents; even the *Meteor* once lost a wire with 8 samplers. By the time much of the work in the Drake Passage was being done, scientists were lowering an electronic package, generally called a CTD, that measures temperature with a platinum resistance thermo-

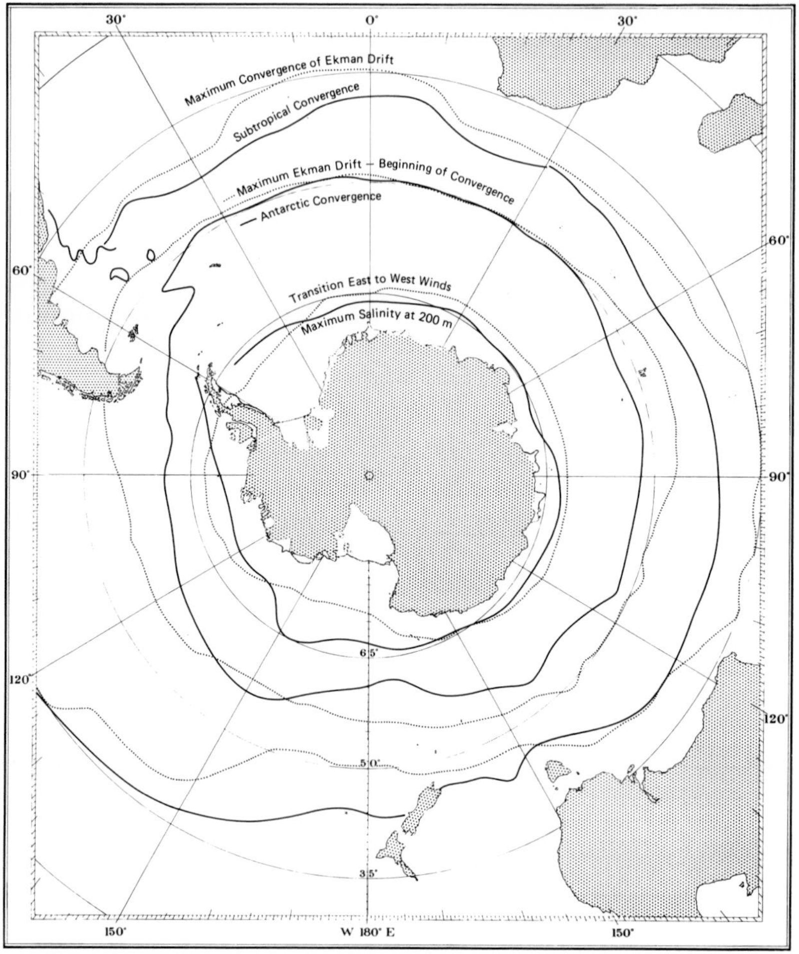

Figure 19
Wind and water boundaries in the
circumpolar ocean

meter, conductivity by an induction method and pressure, for the depth, by a strain gauge technique, and sends all the information up to the ship through the supporting cable so that the observer sees temperature and salinity profiles as the instrument is lowered and raised. It is not quite so easy as it sounds, because the rates of lowering and raising must not be too fast for the sensors, and the different rates of response of the sensors necessitate some computation for the best results, but it makes a tremendous difference to have immediate, continuous information. Water samplers fitted round the electronic package allow the observer in the ship to take samples at critical points on the profile by pushing a button; they also give temperature checks by reversing deep-sea thermometers. At the bottom of the cable there is a 'pinger' that, in conjunction with the ship's echo sounder shows how close the valuable package is to the ocean floor.

The Drake Passage 'dynamic isobars' harmonized with measurements from the current meters indicate large variation in the overall flow, depending more on wide ranging pressure variations than on local winds. The total transport works out at about 130 million metric tons a second. In the near future the partly measured, partly calculated, dynamic topography is likely to be replaced by one measured by radar altimeters in satellites, and we should learn much more about the currents.

North of the west wind region the Trade Winds blow mainly from the south-east. They are most regular on the northern side of the subtropical regions of high pressure centred near 30° S, but they extend farther south near South Africa and Australia, especially in summer. New Zealand stands in the west wind region, though they weaken in North Island particularly in summer. Near Africa and Australia at least, westward water movements begin south of the main Trade Wind belt; some of the water of the Agulhas current flowing south off the east coast of Africa rounds the Cape into the Atlantic Ocean, and there is westward flow round the Australian Bight.

The transition region between the west winds and the east winds near the Antarctic continent is marked by upwelling. North of it the Ekman transport is to the north, and the effect of the earth's rotation on the eastward current makes its density surfaces slope downwards to the north. South of the transition region the opposite occurs, the Ekman transport is to the south and the density surfaces slope downwards to the south. This gives rise to ascending motion between the two regimes to make up for the divergence of flow at the surface. It is always known as the Antarctic divergence, and although it is not a steady feature, the water transports and upwelling being likely to vary with the passing depressions and their varying tracks, its effect on the temperature and salinity distributions is generally clearly marked. The average location of the transition from west to east winds, deduced from charts of annual means of atmospheric pressure, is shown by the dotted line nearest the continent in Figure 19, and that of the circumpolar belt of upwelling, as manifested by a ridge of high salinity in its horizontal distribution at 200 m, is shown by the nearby continuous line.

Away from the region of variable winds near the Antarctic divergence the west wind increases to a maximum in, as far as can be judged from the charts of mean atmospheric pressure, 47° S to 57° S as shown by the second dotted line in Figure 19. The sharpest increase in wind strength occurs some 5 degrees of latitude north of the divergence, and the consequent increase of Ekman transport could be expected to cause more upwelling there, perhaps even more than farther south, where, although the wind changes direction, the meridional gradients of atmospheric pressure are weaker. There are no very positive signs of new upwelling, but it is in these latitudes that the cold tongue of water from the Weddell Sea and a similar, though weaker, one from the Ross Sea become apparent, and these and other irregularities in the near-surface layering may be part of the response to increasing transport.

| Zonation of water types | The following few pages deal with the geographical subdivision of the circumpolar ocean into the three zones, Antarctic, subantarctic and subtropical, suggested by much of the early work. The Antarctic zone extends outwards from the continent to include the colder part of the West Wind Drift. The subantarctic zone, including the warmer part of the West Wind Drift, is a region where the sea and air temperatures increase more sharply to the north. There is generally a particularly sharp transition in temperature and salinity where it converges with water carried southwards in the subtropical region along what has been called the subtropical convergence. |

Climatological charts of sea surface temperature published by meteorological offices are usually based on observations made by ships over many years, averaged over 1 to 5 degree 'squares' – areas bounded by 1 to 5 degrees of latitude and longitude. In the circumpolar ocean they are largely based on data collected before the opening of the Suez and Panama Canals. There are also some painstaking individual studies like that of the Falkland Islands region and Patagonian shelf by Johannes Klaehn, based on some 20 000 observations made by ships rounding Cape Horn before the opening of the Panama Canal in 1914,

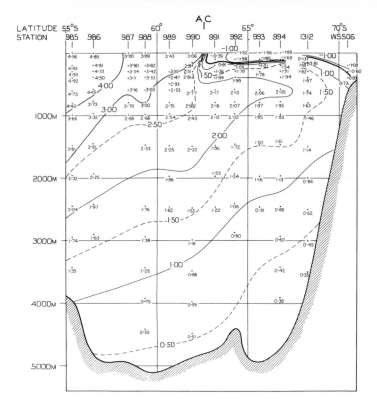
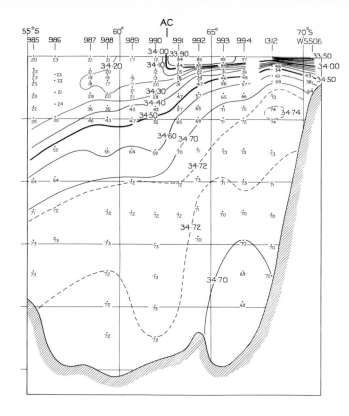

Figure 20
Distribution of temperature (°C) and salinity
(parts per thousand) in a vertical section
through the ocean in 80° W, showing the
different stratification north and south of the
Antarctic convergence

and that compiled by Günther Böhnecke for the Atlantic Ocean from all the available observations. Climatological charts for the circumpolar ocean for each season appear in the *Oceanographical Atlas for the Antarctic* published by the US Navy in 1957, and in the Soviet *Atlas of Antarctica* published in 1966. The averaging over many years and relatively large areas smooths out some small-scale, but important, features and tends to show the surface isotherms as smooth, equally spaced rings round the continent, though somewhat farther north in the Atlantic sector than in the Pacific.

The maps in the new *Southern Ocean Atlas* published in 1982 by Columbia University, made by contouring individual observations, give more realistic seasonal pictures. The surface temperature generally increases, though often irregularly, from the continent, where it is freezing in winter and not far from freezing point in summer, to the Antarctic convergence, where, with a temperature of 1 to 2 °C in winter and 3 to 5 °C in summer, it begins to sink below and mix with warmer water. Where the convergence is far south the temperatures are lower. Figure 20 shows the temperature and salinity distributions in a vertical section along 80° W in the south-east Pacific Ocean. The two southernmost vertical series of observations, on the continental slope, had to be made in summer, but the others were made in October, which is late winter or early spring. The temperature jump from south to north across the convergence, 3 °C, is rather sharper than usual. The most conspicuous feature of the convergence region is the well mixed character of the upper part of the water column on the north side and its sharply stratified character on the south side. There are similar contrasts though at slightly higher temperatures, when the convergence is far north as shown in the section along 30° W, in Figures 21 and 22.

Figure 21
Distribution of temperature in a vertical
section along 30° W

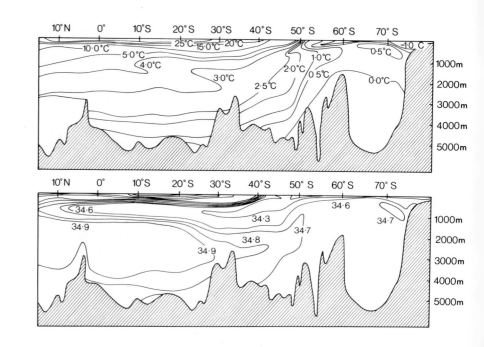

Figure 22
Distribution of salinity (parts per thousand) in
a vertical section along 30° W

The surface stratum of the Antarctic water is warmed in summer. Near the continent the warming begins as soon as the ice cover is removed, and is often accentuated by the trapping of heat in shallow films of water produced by ice melting which lie on the surface because of their low salinity. Farther north the warming is greater, but there is always an underlying nucleus in which the temperature is almost as cold as it was in winter. Below this temperature and salinity increase into the warm deep layer as shown by the higher temperatures and salinities below 200 m in Figures 20, 21 and 22. The cold water at the level of minimum temperature is commonly called 'winter water', but it seems likely that the low temperature is maintained by northward movement from higher latitudes as well as being that of water little affected by summer warming.

The second continuous line in Figure 19, between 49° S and 62° S, shows the position of the Antarctic convergence based on that of the temperature jump at the surface, or the latitude where the temperature minimum of the Antarctic water dips below 200 m as the Antarctic water sinks relatively steeply below the warmer water; both give much the same position. It is not always easy to see the surface temperature jump, but where vertical profiles are available there is no mistaking the pronounced stratification typical of the south side of the convergence or the contrasting uniformity of the well-mixed water on the north side. The boundary is not a steady one, and the line in Figure 19 has been drawn as objectively as possible through points sometimes scattered over 2 or 3 degrees of latitude.

Since the west winds are strongest near the dotted line close to the convergence in Figure 19, and decrease in strength towards the north, the northward Ekman transport must also start to decrease and there

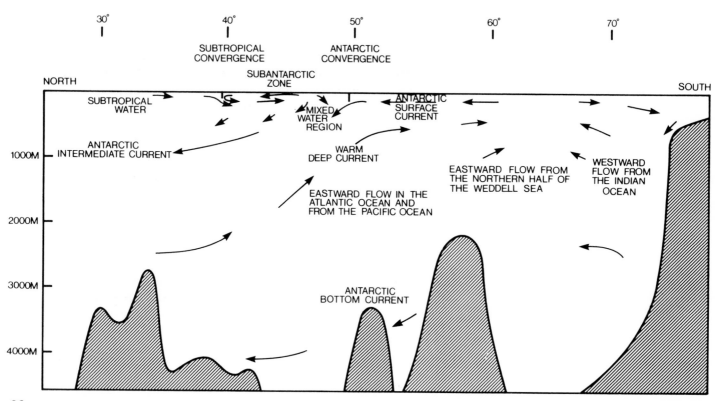

98

must be some tendency towards convergence, but the latitude in which the Antarctic water sinks seems also to depend on the deep and bottom currents and will be discussed again later on.

The fairly sharp rise of temperature suggests that some of the warmth is due to southward flow of water as well as the gradual strengthening of solar radiation, though, since it occurs well within the region of west winds, there must still be northward movement at the surface. Examination of the salinity distribution in vertical north to south sections through the northern part of the west wind region shows, however, that there is generally a subsurface stratum of higher salinity between the surface water and the underlying water that is making its way northwards into the Antarctic intermediate current. It can be seen in Figure 22, and in the schematic diagram of the meridional water circulation in Figure 23 which is based on Figures 21 and 22. It must play some part in warming the mixed water north of the Antarctic convergence. The low salinity of the Antarctic surface water is usually maintained for 1 or 2 degrees north of the convergence, possibly with the help of rainfall, but there is soon a general increase attributable to inflow from the north. The arrival of warmer-water plankton species also indicates some northern influence.

In longitudes where the contrast between the stratified northern part and the well-mixed southern part of the subantarctic zone is most marked the transition between them is accompanied by a sharpening of the temperature gradient at the surface. Günther Böhnecke, one of the *Meteor* scientists, found it about half way between the southern extremities of the Brazil and Agulhas currents and the Antarctic convergence in his map of mean surface temperatures. J. W. Zillman using 43 individual surface profiles south of Australia found a

Figure 23

The main features of meridional water circulation in the section along 30° W, based on the southern parts of Figures 21 and 22. In the circumpolar ocean south of 35° S the water flows mainly east in the west wind region, and west in the east wind region near the Antarctic continent, but there are also important north and southward trends discontinuity averaging 3·6 °C in 80 miles, which was steeper than the gradients he found at the Antarctic and subtropical convergences. Examination of the *Discovery II* and *William Scoresby* thermograph records shows the steepening of surface gradient south of the Brazil and Agulhas currents and south of Australia, but elsewhere it is not clear, or too near the subtropical convergence to be distinguished from it. South of Australia and Africa it begins to be known as the subantarctic front.

The sharpest decrease in the average strength of the west winds occurs near the outermost dotted line in Figure 19, based on annual means of atmospheric pressure. The sharpest northward decrease of Ekman transport must take place there, so that some indication of convergence, with sinking of surface water, could be expected. The continuous line not far away is drawn where there is another sharp increase in temperature towards the north, from about 14 to 18 °C in summer and 11 to 15 °C in winter. There is also a sharp increase in salinity, from about 34·9‰ to 35·4‰. A particularly sharp crossing was observed by the *Meteor* south-east of Cape Town; the convergence was visible from a distance as a line of water disturbance and the surface temperature rose 5·6 °C in 1 mile and 9·1 °C in 5 to 6 miles. The observations on which the line in Figure 19 is based were made in different seasons and over many years and they show some variability, but they probably give its position at any time to within 1 or 2 degrees of latitude, except perhaps in the middle of the oceans where there are relatively few data. The warmer, more saline water must come largely from southward flow in the subtropical region, and there are special conditions south of the strong Brazil, Agulhas and East Australian currents. Patches of warm, highly saline water separate off from the main currents, carrying their physical properties and typical plant and animal populations farther south. South of the Brazil current, for example, the main boundary between the subtropical and subantarctic water types occurs near 43° S but patches of the warm water have reached 48° S. Satellite pictures show the boundary between the cold Falkland current, flowing north along the edge of the Patagonian shelf, and the Brazil current, flowing south farther offshore, to be much more irregular than the average representation obtained by Klaehn from his 20 000 ship observations.

The water boundary is known by the name subtropical convergence, and the full and dotted lines in Figure 19 are sufficiently close together to indicate some association between the water boundary and the maximum convergence of Ekman drift, but there are obviously factors other than the local winds. The change from west to east winds takes place some 5 to 10 degrees farther north, and although the meridional pressure gradients are weaker there sinking of the isotherms to unusually great depths suggests strong downwelling. As near the Antarctic divergence the change in the main direction of flow seems to have more effect than the gradients in Ekman transport. The horizontal and vertical movements near the convergence are not well known, but there is an accumulation of warm water on the north side supplying the subsurface movement on the south side.

Deep circulation   Except in a few areas where they are influenced by prominent topographical features, the deep and bottom waters seem to flow in much the same direction as the surface current, mainly to the east over most of the circumpolar ocean, but to the west along the continental margin, especially where it is far south. The meridional velocities, though emphasized in Figure 23, and playing a very important part in the structure of the ocean and in balancing the net heat loss and fresh-water gain of the Antarctic, are small compared with the zonal speeds. They are too small to be measured directly, and have to be inferred from such information as we possess on the heat and water balances with the atmosphere, and on the drainage, mainly ice, from the land.

The downward slope of the isotherms and isohalines near 50° S in Figures 21 and 22 shows where the Antarctic water begins to sink and mix with warmer water. North of this, weakness of the temperature and salinity gradients shows that there must be a lot of mixing, though in some longitudes a continuation of the Antarctic temperature minimum can be followed quite a long way below the warmer water. Figure 22 shows the striking tongue of low salinity extending northwards from the circumpolar ocean beyond the equator in the west Atlantic basin, and Figure 21 shows that even as far as 10° S its lower part is slightly colder than the underlying more saline water coming from the north Atlantic. This northward extending tongue appears in the report by J. Y. Buchanan, physicist and chemist in HMS *Challenger*, on specific gravities in the ocean, but was not much discussed till demonstrated so convincingly by the *Deutschland* in 1911.

Several names were used: Atlantic intermediate current, subantarctic current and finally Antarctic intermediate current, which seems a good enough description for, although most of the sinking takes place in the mixed-water part of the subantarctic zone, it begins with Antarctic water. The *Meteor* scientists showed that it flows northwards 2 to 5 miles a day in the west Atlantic basin, but more slowly than this in the central and eastern parts of the ocean. Modern oceanographical theory leads one to expect that deep and surface currents are stronger on the western side of the oceans. Some of the intermediate water in the central and eastern parts of the ocean may come from the western marginal flow. There are similar low salinity layers in the Indian and Pacific Oceans, distinguishable almost to the equator, and all round the circumpolar ocean meridional sections show the sinking of Antarctic water, intense mixing north of the convergence and continued sinking of mixed Antarctic and subantarctic waters towards the north. Figure 23 is a schematic picture of these events. Although the northward flow seems to be fastest in the west Atlantic, there is a great accumulation of subantarctic water, and a broad spread of intermediate water in the south-east Pacific. As can be seen in Figure 19 the width of the subantarctic zone increases continuously from the west Atlantic, where it is less than 10 degrees of latitude, to the east Pacific, where it extends over more than 30 degrees.

Since Brennecke found highly saline water extending southwards below the intermediate water in the Atlantic Ocean, and showed that it came from the north Atlantic, it has been known as the North Atlantic deep current. It carries water that sinks from the surface in the Norwegian and Labrador Seas, and, especially in the east Atlantic basin, water whose salinity has been increased by evaporation in the Mediterranean Sea. It remains at a depth of 1500 to 3000 m till it reaches the circumpolar ocean where it rises to the south, above an increasing accumulation of cold bottom water, to a depth of about 250 to 1500 m. It reaches the circumpolar ocean with a temperature of 2·5 to 3 °C, and remains largely between 2 and 1 °C when it joins up with the circumpolar current to form the warm deep layer between the cold surface and bottom layers. Scientists in the USA generally call the warm

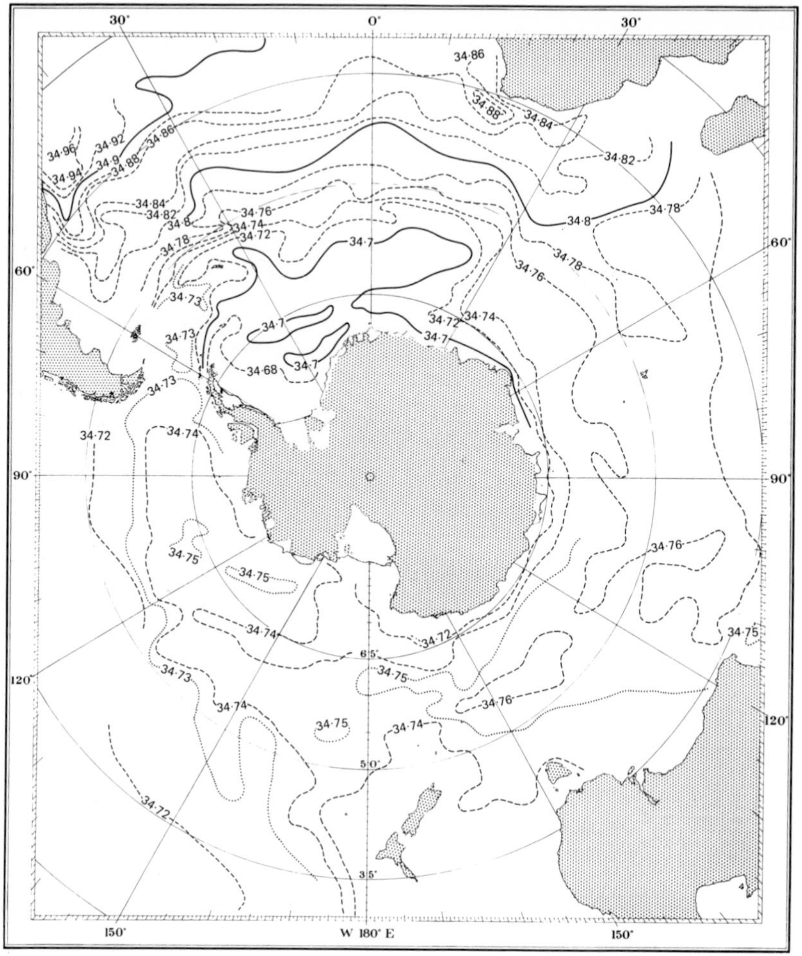

Figure 24
Circumpolar distribution of salinity (parts per
thousand) at the depth of maximum salinity,
based on the Columbia University Southern
Ocean atlas

deep water the circumpolar deep water, though the former name seems more indicative of its northern origin, continuing contrast in temperature and southward trend.

The map reproduced as Figure 24, showing the maximum salinities in the deep water all round the circumpolar ocean, shows that the 34·9‰ isohaline of the North Atlantic deep water reaches to about 35° S in the western Atlantic basin where the southward deep flow, like the northward intermediate flow, is strongest; it reaches to only 20° S in the eastern basin. The 34·80‰ isohaline, after reaching 50° S in the west Atlantic, crosses the ocean near 45° S, and continues far enough into the Indian Ocean to show that a lot of the North Atlantic deep water rounds the Cape of Good Hope. Farther east the maximum salinity decreases continuously round the circumpolar ocean, though with many minor variations likely to be due to local singularities in vertical mixing or inflows of less saline water. By the time the circumpolar current reaches the Drake Passage the maximum salinity is reduced to 34·73‰, the decrease being due mainly to the transfer of salt to the surface and bottom currents and their northward movements, balancing the effect of fresh water added from the excess of precipitation over evaporation, and, being by then almost the densest water in the ocean, contributing largely to northward bottom flow, especially in the Pacific Ocean.

It is useful to distinguish between the upper part of the warm deep water where the maximum temperature occurs, and the lower part that has the maximum salinity. There is a southward movement and rise in salinity below the Antarctic intermediate water in all the oceans, although the Pacific Ocean has no source of highly saline water like that feeding the North Atlantic deep current, and the Indian Ocean only a relatively small one. It seems likely that much of the warmer part of the

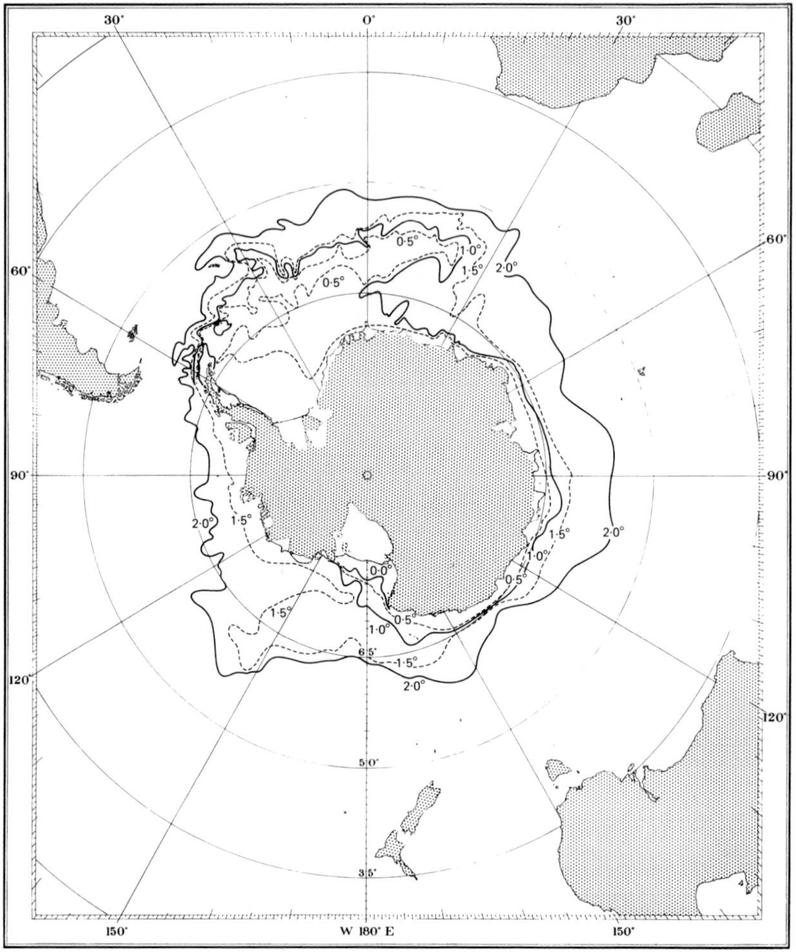

Figure 25
Circumpolar distribution of temperature (°C)
at the depth of maximum temperature

deep water must be intermediate water turning back to the south after mixing with underlying water in warmer latitudes. In the Atlantic Ocean it must mix with the North Atlantic deep water, in the Indian Ocean with mixtures of deep water from the north and bottom water from the south, and in the Pacific Ocean with deep water that seems to be derived mainly from northward bottom flow from the circumpolar ocean.

Although the North Atlantic current has such a recognizable effect on the lower part of the deep water, the warmth of the upper part must be maintained by southward movement all round the circumpolar ocean. There is much to be learnt about such movements, and their differences from one sector to another. They may partly be compensating for surface transport to the north in the region of west winds, and partly maintaining a density equilibrium between the colder waters formed in the south and warmer waters farther north. Arnold Gordon, striking a balance between the salt and heat carried south by the deep current and the losses of heat and gains of fresh water expected in the Antarctic, estimated that the total southward movement, all round the circumpolar ocean, is 77 million metric tons a second, more than half the zonal transport of the circumpolar current, and of this the North Atlantic deep current contributes only an estimated 15 million metric tons a second. Although the south and north transports are quite large in total, they require only very small rates of flow over the range of depths and great horizontal distances involved, too small to be measured directly.

Close to the Antarctic continent where the winds come from the east and the surface water flows to the west, the deep and bottom currents show the same trend. It is particularly evident south of the Atlantic Ocean and in the Weddell Sea, where Brennecke, combining his own observations with those of the French, Swedish and Scottish expeditions, showed that the deep water near the southern margin is significantly warmer than that in the northern part of the sea, and demonstrated that there must be a westward flow along the continental margin from the south-west Indian sector. It is shown very clearly in the map of maximum temperatures in the warm deep layer drawn in Figure 25. The warm deep water moves clockwise round the Weddell Sea and after a lot of mixing with the cold surface and bottom waters comes out much modified to cross the Atlantic with a temperature less than 0·5 °C. There is a similar, though weaker, circulation in the deep water north of the Ross Sea.

Everywhere the maximum temperature and thickness of the warm layer decrease near the continent as the warm layer mixes more and more with the colder overlying and underlying waters, and in most longitudes its temperature falls below 0 °C before it reaches the 1000 m contour on the continental slope; only in the south-east Pacific and south-west Indian Oceans, where the deep water seems warmer than usual, does water warmer than 0 °C reach on to the continental shelf. The deep current, being the only southward movement, has to replace much of the water carried by the northward movements in the surface and bottom layers. It is easy to see how it can gain the characteristics of the surface water: mixing, surface cooling, excess of precipitation over evaporation, ice melting and drainage from the continent, afford a ready explanation for the change of its temperature of 2 °C and salinity of 34·7‰, to the minus temperatures and 34·0‰ salinity of the surface water. Its transformation to bottom water is not so readily explained since the bottom water though much colder than the deep water is only a little less saline. To gain such properties the deep water must mix with cold water of relatively high salinity; nowhere, certainly not on any large scale, does it become exposed at the surface to direct cooling by radiation.

Although, except in a few places, the warm deep water does not reach on to the continental shelf with a temperature higher than 0 °C, and the circulation on the shelf – in the east wind region – is probably mainly southwards at the surface and northwards at the bottom, the shelf loses water to the surface and bottom currents farther north, and much of this has to be made good by the southward movement in the warm deep layer. T. D. Foster in the US icebreaker *Glacier* in 1968 found a tongue of modified deep water crossing the shelf break near 51° W in the south-western Weddell Sea, its maximum temperature decreasing from 0·21 to −0·15 °C and its salinity at the same depths from 34·66 to 34·62‰ as the sounding shallowed from 3265 to 695 m. There seem to be similar incursions on to the shelf at the head of canyons reaching up the continental slope north of the Ross Sea.

All round the circumpolar continental shelf the water must become almost uniform with depth in winter, at freezing or near-freezing temperature and with a salinity increased by the salt left behind as ice is formed. Although the most saline water approaching the Ross Sea from the north has a salinity of 34·74‰, summer observations show that most of the water below 250 m in the western part of the shelf basin has a salinity higher than this, reaching 34·92‰ at the bottom, and the effect is likely to be more widespread before summer melting begins. This might have been realized from Nelson's samples in 1911–12 if they had received the attention they deserved, or from others collected by E. H. Marshall, ship's surgeon in the whaling factory *C. A. Larsen* in 1928–29 in a spell between his voyages in the old *Discovery* and the new *Discovery*

109

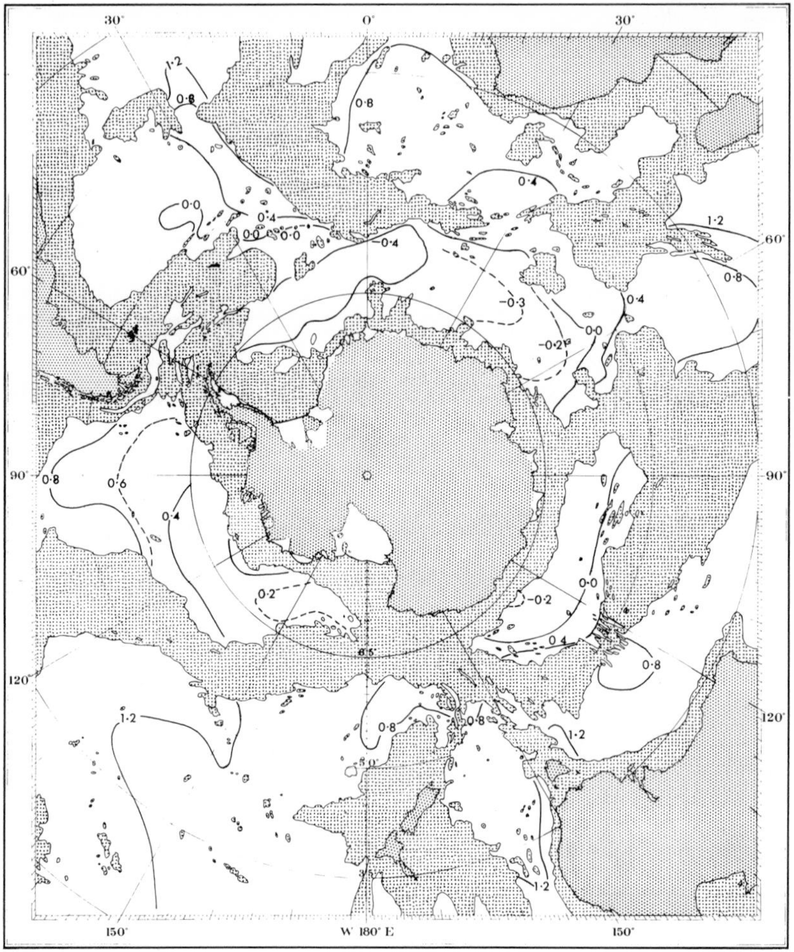

Figure 26
Temperature (°C) of the bottom water at
depths greater than 4000 m. Soundings less
than 4000 m are shaded

II, if the scientists at home had not suspected them. However, it was not really recognized till the *Discovery II* made a survey of the area in 1936 after 'rescuing' the American flyer Lincoln Ellsworth.

Sea water near its freezing point, approximately −1·9 °C, and with a salinity greater than 34·51‰ can form mixtures with the deep water sufficiently dense to sink below it. This is how most of the bottom water is formed – by mixing near the shelf edge. It does not happen south of the Pacific Ocean where, as far as we can judge from the 'winter water' in the Antarctic temperature minimum, the salinity of the shelf water is always too low. A lot of cold, highly-saline, water is formed in the Ross Sea but its sinking down the continental slope seems to be much restricted by a submarine ridge that separates the shelf basin from the deep ocean outside; some escapes but apparently rather little compared with the sinking from the shelf south and west of the Weddell Sea.

Figure 26 contours the temperatures of the bottom water at depths greater than 4000 m. The coldest water extends eastwards across the Atlantic sector from the continental slope east of the Antarctic Peninsula. There is then a general rise in temperature towards the east, with only small signs of new supplies of cold water near 130° E.

Figure 27 shows summer conditions between 130° E and 133° E. As in most longitudes the soundings rise from the deep ocean to 200–300 m at the edge of the continental shelf and then deepen into a shelf basin before rising slowly to the continent. The deeper part of the shelf basin is filled with water whose low temperature and high salinity are typical of the previous winter. The surface water is slightly warmed and diluted by solar heating and ice melting. Outside the shelf there is clear evidence of the shelf water mixing with the warm deep water approaching from the north and sinking below it. There are a number of

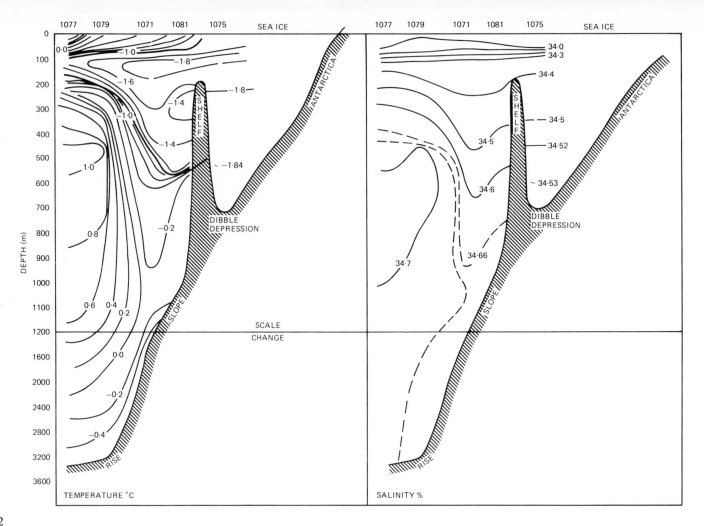

112

forces likely to promote and assist mixing near the continental slope: the effect of the change in depth on the tides and current will produce eddying disturbances, and variations of flow associated with the passage of depressions farther north must have a considerable influence. The low temperature of the bottom water issuing from the Weddell Sea and the general rise in temperature towards the east give a clear indication that the Weddell Sea is the major source, and except for the sinking of water from the shelf between the Ross Sea and 130° E there are no obvious reinforcements, though the intensive cooling all round the continental margin must play some part in maintaining the bottom water flow.

The bottom water spreads northwards in the Atlantic, Indian and Pacific Oceans, and it is remarkable that in the west Atlantic basin the temperature at the bottom near the equator is about the same as that near the Antarctic Circle in the east Pacific Ocean. Arnold Gordon estimates that the total northward bottom flow, all round the circumpolar ocean, is 34 million metric tons a second, about a quarter of the circumpolar current, and Bruce Warren points out that it is the major source of cold water in ocean depths farther north. There is some evidence from current measurements, and photographs of ripples and other small features in the surface of the bottom sediments, that the water movement is in much the same direction as the surface and deep currents, and the measurements indicate that passing changes of current direction at the surface are accompanied by similar changes at the bottom. The relatively warm bottom temperatures along the continental margin south of the Atlantic Ocean, compared with those extending eastwards from the northern part of the Weddell Sea, give a clear indication of westward bottom flow in the region of east winds.

Figure 27
Temperature and salinity distributions in a vertical section across the continental slope near 132° E, showing the influence of cold, poorly saline, shelf water on the deep water farther north (after A. L. Gordon and P. Tchernia)

113

Since the water on the Antarctic shelf is colder and more saline in winter it is reasonable to suppose that most bottom water will be formed then. There are too few observations, too widely distributed in time and space, to check this probability, but, except for the work of Brennecke, all the evidence we have of cold water sinking down the continental slope has been obtained in summer, and A. E. Gill has pointed out that the effect of the earth's rotation, tending to move the surface water to the left of the current, is likely to keep the cold water on the shelf till overcome by other factors. T. D. Foster's observations show active sinking down the continental slope east of the Antarctic Peninsula; there is an accumulation of cold, highly-saline, surface water round the northern end of the peninsula, attributable to northward flow in the Weddell Sea; there is nothing like it farther south down the west coast. It must influence conditions in the Bransfield Strait which are more severe than those farther south, and those of the mixed-water region between the Drake Passage and Weddell Sea currents.

The Antarctic convergence

The deep and bottom currents, particularly the relatively steep climb of the deep water over a thickening wedge of bottom water half way across the circumpolar ocean, seem to be important among the factors that determine the latitude where the Antarctic surface water begins to sink below warmer water. One has to bear in mind that diagrams like Figures 21, 22 and 23 have to be drawn with a vertical exaggeration of about 600 to print them on a page, and the steepest slopes of general trends of the isotherms and density surfaces are all less than 1 in 100, but the vertical displacements over a few hundred miles are quite large, enough to afford scope for convection.

In a simpler situation, without the salinity layering, cold water might be expected to sink in the south and be replaced by warmer water flowing in from the north. In the presence of the warm deep water, which although warm is denser than the surface water because of its higher salinity, the cold water cannot sink far vertically, but it can deepen gradually towards the north till it reaches the latitudes where the deep water and its density surfaces are emerging from much greater depths and then sink more freely. As explained earlier, the transition region where the Antarctic surface water slips below and mixes with warmer water is marked by a sharp rise in temperature towards the north, and if only vertical series of observations are available there is no mistaking the stratification and shallow temperature minimum of the south side, or the deeper uniformity of the north side. The most remarkable feature of the convergence of the warm and cold waters is the constancy of its mean position. The surface temperature jump is usually found very close to where the Antarctic temperature minimum, turning sharply downwards, sinks below 200 m; these were the criteria used in plotting the line in Figure 19, and a comparison with 200 crossings showed that half were within 60 miles of the mean position shown on the map, and less than a tenth as much as 120 miles away. The early observations, though they showed variations of 60 miles or so on either side of a probable mean position, called attention to the wonder of such a relatively stable feature in the middle of a wide ocean, apparently continuous round the circumpolar ocean. Perhaps too little attention was paid to the variability, but today, when closely spaced observations and continuously recording instruments are telling us so much more about meanders and eddies that vary the surface conditions, and interleaving of warm and cold strata below the surface, perhaps too little attention is being paid to the overall significance of the transition region.

Some of the reported variability is a consequence of different criteria being used to define it. A favourite alternative is to use the latitude where the sinking Antarctic water leads to a minimum salinity at the 200 m level; this generally occurs several degrees of latitude north of where the colder, more saline water of the Antarctic temperature minimum sinks, and includes varying effects of mixing and exchanges with the atmosphere north of the first sinking point. In the Drake Passage, the convergence as plotted by infra-red measurements from a satellite varies irregularly 1 or 2 degrees of latitude on either side of the line in Figure 19, but agrees closely with it on average.

There are some differences in the choice of name. Schott called it the Meinardus line. Defant and Wüst, in the late 1920s, changed to Oceanic Polar Front and, thinking of it as a dividing line between mainly Antarctic and recognizably tropical influences, like the meteorologist's Polar Front, plotted it farther north than Meinardus. The *Discovery* scientists in the early 1930s, wanting to refer as simply as possible to the surface transition from cold to warm waters and from typically Antarctic to manifestly warmer-water plankton species that could reasonably be described as subantarctic, used the name Antarctic convergence. In recent years the name Polar Front is again being used though with some uncertainty; it began with the use of Polar Front Zone to cover a zone 3 or 4 degrees wide over which the transition was believed to vary, but now this name is broadened to include the well-mixed water zone north of where the Antarctic water begins to sink, and 'Polar Front' is kept for the zone of minimum salinity at 200 m, which itself is several degrees north of where the Antarctic water begins to sink and where there is a clear transition in physical and chemical properties and plankton species. The former terminology seems simpler and perhaps more representative.

The long-term stability of the mean position is perhaps not very surprising if it is associated with such slowly changing things as the long-term pattern of heat and water exchanges with the atmosphere, the mean winds and the deep and bottom currents, and some dependence of these currents on the bottom topography. South of Australia the convergence apparently lines up with the mid-ocean ridge, partly, perhaps, because of the effect of the ridge on the zonal current, and also its possible ponding of the bottom water to the south and the influence of this on the latitude where the warm deep water climbs much nearer the surface. It would be useful to know just why the convergence is so far north in the Atlantic sector and so far south in the eastern Pacific. The great flow of cold water from the Weddell Sea, itself largely attributable to the presence of the Antarctic Peninsula, deflecting the westward flow near the continent, must be the main cause. The Ross Sea, whose west coast does not extend so far north, and which produces a smaller volume of bottom water, has a much smaller effect, though its cold water, as well as the mid-ocean ridge, is probably responsible for the marked northward advance of the current and the convergence in 150° W to 140° W. The presence of calcareous sediments above siliceous sediments north of the present position of the convergence indicates that it has retreated southwards since the last ice age, but close agreement between the surface temperatures measured by James Clark Ross and those of today give a clear indication that its position has not changed much over the past 150 years.

The temperature contrast between the Weddell Sea current and the

water flowing through the Drake Passage, though weakening towards the east, is recognizable across the Atlantic sector. Between the South Shetland and South Orkney Islands there is a sharp front between the two currents, with a narrow region of cold water that separates them at all depths; the separation between the substantial warm deep layer to the north and the much modified deep water that has circulated round the Weddell Sea is particularly remarkable. The front seems to be associated with the southern arm of the Scotia Arc, and continues along it to the east before curving northwards past the South Sandwich group, sending a cold tongue to the north-west off the north-east coast of South Georgia, and continuing eastwards across the Atlantic Ocean. East of the South Orkneys, however, its position seems variable; a recent survey by the US research ship *Melville* showed no well-defined boundary, though it seems fairly clear as a climatic feature when all the available data are averaged, and there is always a tongue of cold water north-east of South Georgia, and, in exceptional years, typical Weddell Sea ice.

Sea ice

However violently a very cold sea surface is agitated by wind and waves this does not prevent it freezing. Patches of ice crystals, appearing smooth like patches of oil, are formed among the waves, and as they spread the roughness calms to a smooth swell. The multiplying crystals form a sludge over the whole surface, often helped by snow-fall, and slowly coagulate into pancake ice, small, flat round plates raised round the edges by jostling and splashing. Later on, or farther south, the pancakes grow to larger size, 10 to 15 feet in diameter, retaining their pancake shape, and soft and sticky with salt till covered with snow. As freezing continues and the ice is depressed by the weight of snow most

Figure 28
The sea beginning to freeze, 68½° S 91° W, 8 March 1934

one-year ice grows to a thickness of 3 to 5 feet, though in a high-latitude area like McMurdo Sound, where the ice remains fixed through a long winter, it is likely to be twice as thick, and strong enough for heavy aircraft to land on.

Going south in summer a ship is likely to meet outlying streams of small snow-covered floes and broken ice, and to see ahead the bright sky known as ice blink where the clouds are whitened by reflection from the more continuous ice, sometimes with one or two patches of darker sky above leads of open water. It is then that she comes to a dazzling white and blue seascape, often of calm water, in which the main body of pack ice emerges as a white line along the horizon. Its edge is fairly compact, but irregular and variable. It begins with a fringe of small floes where most of the wave energy is expended and in bad weather, churning fragments are a danger to ships; there are many accounts of its dangers in Cook's and Ross's voyages. Only longer, lower waves penetrate far into the ice, where the floes are less broken, and the movements smaller and less violent. Whaling factories always operated near the ice edge when they could, being sheltered by outlying ice tongues, though in bad weather they had to go farther in, or away from the ice altogether, to escape the turmoil of churning fragments.

At the end of winter 60 per cent of the ocean south of the Antarctic convergence, an area greater than the Antarctic continent, is covered with ice but most of it melts in summer till only about 12 per cent remains covered. During the past 20 years satellite-monitored radiation in the infra-red, visual and microwave bands has added much to previous studies of the position of the ice edge as reported by ships, and daily reports of ice distribution and density are available to ships making their way through it. Its northward advance in winter depends on the

Figure 29
Pancake ice and old ice in 64°40′ S 127° E, south of Australia, 20 March 1936, with some appearance of land on the horizon

winds and currents as well as the latitude and height of the sun. The south winds and northward current along the east side of the Antarctic Peninsula carry the ice to 55° S between South Georgia and Bouvet Island. It is found north of South Georgia in exceptional years and makes Bouvet unapproachable in winter. Farther east it tends to recede till in the east Pacific sector the winter northern limit is about 65° S, though the retreat seems to be lessened near the Kerguelen plateau and north of the Balleny Islands, and there is a significant advance between 150° W and 140° W, probably partly attributable to cold water from the Ross Sea. The tongue of cold water and ice carried across the Atlantic in 58° S to 63° S by the current from the Weddell Sea is still carrying ice when it has all melted north of 65° S in other longitudes.

The northern limit in winter varies only a few degrees from year to year, the variations being greatest north of the Weddell and Ross Seas where northward transport of ice from large areas farther south seems to be important, and least where the continent extends far north. The overall ice cover generally reaches its maximum by the middle of September, though it may be a month or so later in the Atlantic sector because of the transfer of ice from the Weddell Sea. It falls to its minimum by the middle of February, the melting taking less time than the freezing. The water has its minimum and maximum temperatures in these same months. The ice edge advances most rapidly in May and June, and retreats most rapidly in November and December. Some parts of the coast are reasonably accessible to shipping from late December to March; the most inaccessible coasts are the western margin of the Weddell Sea, where the wind and current packs the ice against the Antarctic Peninsula, and south of the Pacific Ocean, where the persistence of heavy ice near the coast has been attributed to outflow of

Figure 30
Heavy pack ice in 69½° S 100° W, near Captain Cook's farthest south, 6 January 1931

123

cold air from the continent. Heavy multi-year ice is found in such areas.

Satellite observations give some indication that the density of ice cover within the northern ice edge – the proportion of ice to open water – may be less than was supposed: even in winter half of the area seems to be only 85 per cent covered, and a further quarter only 65 per cent covered. There is, however, much uncertainty about these figures because the heavy burden of snow may be sufficient to depress the ice below sea level and let in enough salt to make some of the ice look like water to microwave frequencies. Antarctic bases have often reported open water near the coast when offshore winds drive the ice out to sea; satellite pictures show ice-free areas farther offshore. The most frequent is a large irregular area, sometimes about 800 miles long, varying between 10° E and 25° W in 58° S to 65° S, in the south-east approach to the Weddell Sea. It is probably associated with inflow of warmer water from the south-west Indian sector and with upwelling between the East and West Wind Drifts. Cook found open water between these latitudes after he had rounded the Weddell ice tongue extending 1000 miles farther east between 55° S and 60° S, and Brennecke showed that there must be a westward movement of warm water in the deep layer. The area of open water, often seen in satellite pictures, is known as the Weddell polynya, the name polynya being derived from the Russian word for a space of open water in the middle of Arctic ice. It does not have open water every winter, but the area seems always to be the last to freeze and the first to melt, making the Weddell Sea more approachable from the east. Another large area opens in the southern Ross Sea in early summer, probably because the winds blow the ice offshore, but there is some indication, particularly in the deep temperature charts, of a clockwise circulation like that of the Weddell

Sea though on a much smaller scale. The occurrence and positioning of heavy and weak ice areas vary sufficiently to influence plans for re-supplying land bases, and make the satellite pictures very useful; day to day changes in wind patterns often produce dangerous pressure areas.

Much attention is being paid to the probable effects of the varying ice cover on regional and global climate, particularly its influence on the balance of incoming and outgoing radiation and the transfer of heat and water vapour. South of the Indian Ocean a recession of 2·5 degrees in the latitude of the ice edge has been associated with an increase of 1 °C in the mean annual temperature at the Antarctic coast. There is a relation between mean annual temperature and duration of ice cover at the South Orkney Islands, and between the mean temperature and nearness of ice at South Georgia. It seems likely that the ice limits influence the paths of depressions travelling eastwards, and there is some indication that a major ice advance in one sector is accompanied by less ice in another, usually opposite, sector.

Pack ice beginning to melt in spring and summer is conspicuously discoloured by phytoplankton growth near water level, where, in rather porous ice, there is sufficient light transmitted through the snow and ice cover to allow photosynthesis, and a sufficient supply of nutrients from the sea water. It is probably a favourable environment; in the open water outside, vertical mixing may seriously reduce the time that the plants remain near the surface in light strong enough to support growth and reproduction, whereas in the ice they are kept at a level of adequate illumination. It has been suggested that they may be important in maintaining the high annual production in Antarctic waters, though the large phytoplankton blooms that turn the sea green near the ice edge do

not occur till the ice melts and the surface water is fully exposed to sunlight; rapid growth is then likely to be favoured by the thin layer of melt water that increases the stability near the surface and helps to keep the phytoplankton in the well-illuminated upper levels.

In very high latitudes like those of the Ross and Weddell Seas, where the water becomes so cold that it cannot lose more heat without freezing, and lines and fish traps left in the water are coated with ice crystals, the ice crystals also appear to contribute to the underside of the ice cover. The observations in McMurdo Sound show that in shallow soundings ice also forms on the bottom, and when this 'ground ice' or 'anchor ice' becomes detached it carries bottom-living animals to the underside of the ice cover, and eventually they may become exposed on the surface. Scott's northern sledging parties reported sandy patches with the remains of marine animals; on a number of occasions they came upon headless fishes, presumably they had floated and become incorporated in the underside of the ice after their heads had been bitten off by seals. US scientists working with ice-cores from the Weddell Sea recently found that the lower 50 per cent of the core was composed of consolidated ice crystals.

Icebergs

Edmond Halley's awe-struck account of the icebergs north of South Georgia in January 1700 seems to be the first Antarctic record. Captain Cook saw 'ice islands' all round the circumpolar ocean; he concluded that they were formed of consolidated snow on land farther south, and separated from its ice cliffs. Those with a flat, even surface must, he thought, be formed in the bays and flat valleys, and the more irregular ones near rocky and mountainous coasts. The large 'tabular' icebergs are

Figure 31
Corner of tabular iceberg 75 feet high, between the South Orkney and South Shetland Islands showing water-worn stratification, 18 December 1930

a unique feature of the Antarctic ocean. In January 1927 the Norwegian whale-catcher *Odd I* reported steaming 90 miles along the north face of a tabular berg 100–130 feet high near Clarence Island in the South Shetland group, and in the following month the *Discovery* reported the sea south of Clarence Island to be crowded with enormous tabular bergs, one of which extended across the whole horizon. At about the same time the whaling factory *Lancing* reported a berg as large as South Georgia lying 100 miles north-east of the South Orkney Islands.

In October of the same year the merchant ships *Orita* and *Winterhude* reported many bergs, one of them 10 miles long, transported to the region between the Falkland Islands and the River Plate, and in December the whaling transport *Tijuca* reported bergs in sight all the way from South Georgia to the River Plate, one of them 'understood to be 50 miles long'. On 11–13 February, two months later, the *William Scoresby* worked a station, and sheltered for two days in the lee of a large iceberg estimated to be 70 miles long half way between the Falkland Islands and South Georgia. Such large outbreaks of ice seem to be comparatively rare, but another large berg 60–70 miles long was reported by the *Discovery II* between South Georgia and the South Sandwich Islands in February 1930, and three months later the *William Scoresby* found one 45 miles long 100 miles north of South Georgia, possibly part of the same one. There were more in the following year between Clarence Island and the South Sandwich Islands adding to the impression that they must be carried by the Weddell Sea current from the large ice shelves we now know to exist south of the Atlantic Ocean.

Scientists of the British Antarctic Survey, the US National Environment Satellite Service and the Scott Polar Research Institute, have now followed the history of large icebergs on pictures taken by US satellites.

Figure 32
Cape Bowles, Clarence Island, 13 November 1936

129

In September 1967 a large iceberg seen drifting to the west along the Antarctic coast was identified with a glacier tongue previously photographed in 1° W, and now found to be missing, having apparently been struck by another large iceberg travelling westwards. From 12° W where it was first sighted it travelled to 48° W where it grounded near the coast and remained for five years. It was then 56 miles long and 32 miles wide. Starting off again, embedded in pack ice, it reached the tip of the Antarctic Peninsula two years later, by which time it had calved several major fragments, and its size was reduced to 50 × 27 miles. It then headed generally northwards in open water and passed east of Clarence Island into the Scotia Sea. By March 1978 it was just west of South Georgia, having lost little more in size. It crossed 50° S in 40° W in April 1978 and then moved mainly east. It was identified every few days from April to June in pictures taken by a newly developed very-high-resolution radiometer, and was seen to circle round a submarine seamount. By this time, nearly 11 years since it was first identified, it was reduced in size to about 30 × 12 miles, a fifth of its original area.

There are a few ice islands in the Arctic derived from ice shelves in northern Ellesmere Island and northern Greenland, but in the Antarctic nearly all the bergs in the coastal region are large and flat topped. Their vertical sides show visible stratification, the top layers being hard packed snow with a density only about half that of ice. The density increases with depth till at 150 feet or so the properties are those of hard, impermeable, ice, but it is ice that contains 3 to 8 per cent of small bubbles of compressed air from the layers of compressed snow of which it was formed. There are also crevasses in the tabular bergs, some opening downwards as well as the more usual deep fissures at the surface. The most common height of tabular bergs seems to be 100 to

Figure 33
Looking southwards over the Weddell Sea from John Peak (1361 feet), Powell Island, South Orkney Islands, 4 January 1932

131

150 feet though 200 feet is sometimes reported. Their depth below water is 4 to 5 times this – less than the 9 times that would be expected if they were all solid ice.

Wave action undercuts the ice cliffs, which collapse into the water, and there is sometimes a terrace left jutting out below the surface. Scientists from the Scott Polar Research Institute have measured the rolling and pitching of icebergs with the help of sensitive instruments fixed by Navy helicopters. The icebergs respond mainly to long waves, and possibly to differences between high and low groups of waves, and tend to oscillate at their own natural frequencies dependent on their stability, size and shape. A tabular berg measuring approximately 2×1 miles was found to tilt up to one tenth of a degree. Such strains are believed to be an important factor in causing calving and break up. Icebergs are not held by pack ice but charge through it, or if a strong wind is blowing the pack ice charges past the berg; in such conditions there is heavy ice pressure to windward of the berg and a wake of open water behind it.

Within 100 or 200 miles of the Antarctic coastline between 50 and 200 icebergs are likely to be visible from the ship at any time, and close inshore the ship may have to manoeuvre through closer assemblages. They are likely to be encountered as far north as the Antarctic convergence, especially where they are carried northwards from the Weddell and Ross Seas, and near the Kerguelen plateau, where Tchernia found that all his monitored icebergs travelling westwards along the coast turned north. South of Cape Town the *Discovery* found a concentration of icebergs in 58° S to 63° S in the path of the current from the Weddell Sea. In the West Wind Drift most icebergs show signs of decay. Melting seems to take place more rapidly under the surface

Figure 34
Weathered iceberg in the Bellingshausen Sea,
30 December 1930

where ice and water are in contact and, becoming unstable, the berg tilts to expose water-worn surfaces, and sometimes rolls right over. Calving sometimes makes them take on fantastic shapes before they eventually fall apart. The early explorers found no copious flows of melt water like those they had tapped from Arctic icebergs. Few icebergs are seen north of the Antarctic convergence except in extreme years like 1927–28.

Icebergs containing dark coloured layers, ranging from black to bottle green, are sometimes seen, mostly north and north-east of the Weddell Sea but also as far as 100° W in the Bellingshausen Sea. The black ice is opaque and carries mud and stones, and some organic matter, the sort of detritus that might collect on the surface of a glacier or be frozen into its underside if it scours the sea floor or incorporates ground ice like that known in McMurdo Sound. At the surface the contaminating material might be wind deposited following volcanic activity not very far away. This seems likely because the boundary between the dark and white parts of the berg is clearly a plane; though one layer is blackened the next is white. The bottle-green bergs appear more translucent and contaminated with less and finer material; they may be the result of less severe deposition. A most remarkable feature is that the dark part is invariably smoothly rounded by water action; no one appears to have seen a dark band in the side of a tabular berg.

The total volume of ice present in drifting and grounded bergs at any one time has been estimated at 8×10^{12} m³, and the amount liberated each year from the continent as $1\cdot3 \times 10^{12}$ m³. It suggests that icebergs last on an average about six years, which seems reasonable from the relatively little we know of them. Although, as just mentioned, a large iceberg has been tracked for 11 years, others escaping more quickly to warmer water are not likely to last so long. The possibility of towing

Figure 35
Weathered iceberg south-east of South
Georgia, 3 April 1931

136

icebergs to arid countries as potential sources of fresh water, now being investigated, has promoted new interest in the problems of their formation, distribution and decay, as well as the formidable mechanical difficulties of towing and mooring such enormous masses.

Side-scan sonar techniques used on continental shelves and slopes round the Arctic ocean show criss-cross patterns of furrows some 60 feet wide and 6 feet deep that have been ploughed into the sea floor by moving icebergs. Known as iceberg scours, or just ploughmarks, they are found in the Davis Strait and Labrador Sea, and, as a relic of former iceberg activity, west of the British Isles and off the coast of Norway. Side-scan has not yet been exploited much on the Antarctic shelf and slope, but the Norwegian research ship *Polarsirkel* found ploughmarks extending down to 350 m south of the Weddell Sea. Perhaps the deepest of these might be relics of a former era of lower sea level.

Underwater noise from melting icebergs is sufficient to attract considerable interest. There can be occasional sharp noises due to stresses and strains, but also a continuous noise which, at the common listening frequencies, sounds like frying fat. The main source is probably the melting and bursting of the small air bubbles in the ice which are believed to have pressures up to 20 atmospheres, though wave noise may also be significant. Another source of noise in melting glacier ice was described by Professor Tyndall the well-known alpinist; he attributed the clinking sounds from a block of glacier ice held in front of a glowing fire to the water melting round dust particles and drawing sharply from the walls of a cavity that would be slightly larger than the volume of water. E. H. Smith of the International Ice Patrol, set up in the north Atlantic after the sinking of the *Titanic*, found that the icebergs were noisier in bright sunlight than during the night. Ships passing close

Figure 36
Morainic iceberg near South Georgia, 1 April 1930

137

to icebergs see a band of noise on their echo-sounding records, and horizontal directional receivers have detected the noise at distances of 50 to 100 miles. It has been suggested that plankton, fish and mammals are attracted by the noise. There is also much underwater noise near a pack-ice boundary, probably due to wave noise and the pieces clashing together.

It has been thought likely that icebergs might be detected by lowering of sea surface temperature, but their effect depends very much on the roughness of the sea. In calm sheltered water melt water is likely to produce a thin, stable, surface layer that absorbs much of the solar heating; under such conditions higher surface temperatures have been measured near icebergs. In contrast there seems to be no clear evidence of cooling in the rougher, more mixed, water near a berg in the open ocean.

Waves and swell

The 'roaring forties' are notorious for high waves though it is doubtful whether they are worse than those of north Atlantic or north Pacific winters. Early sailors while being careful to report the strength of the wind did not often particularize about the waves. Halley did not describe them, though he wrote about gentle, moderate, fresh, stout and very hard gales. Captain Cook mentioned 'prodigious high seas' and 'large swell'. Captain Henry Foster on his way to Deception Island in HMS *Chanticleer* wrote 'The depth to which the waves rise and fall is still a matter of speculation, some attributing it to six feet rise and six feet fall, and others again according to their own individual observation or their ideas of the bounds of probability. I have heard many experienced practical seamen estimate it at thirty feet, nor does this appear to me in the least degree an exaggeration.' Robert Fitzroy, captain of HMS *Beagle*, remarked on the complacency of landlubbers who set 30 feet as the maximum height of storm waves; he had seen waves twice that high. Dumont d'Urville reported that he had encountered waves 100 feet high on his voyages. William Scoresby measured waves up to 43 feet high in the west wind region on his way to Australia in 1856. HMS *Challenger* experienced some of the strongest winds of her voyage between the Crozet Islands and Kerguelen, but John Murray in his account of the marine fauna of the Kerguelen region, while noting that the waves during this period were the highest of the voyage, gives their height as only 23 feet.

The *Challenger* officers, like most seamen, seem to have been rather casual about reporting 'sea state', the appropriate column in the meteorological record has some long blanks, and the figures given for rough water now seem to be underestimates. When the observer climbs to a deck high enough to get the wave crests in line with the horizon with the ship on an even keel the measurement is likely to be reliable, but it is difficult to get a reliable figure by judging the general appearance of the sea. The continuous records of wave height now available from shipborne instruments have given a more perceptible picture of the irregularities of a normal wave pattern, and to convey a representative impression it has become the custom to report not the highest wave, or the average of all the waves, but the average of the highest third, and this over a 20-minute record is known as the 'significant wave height'. The maximum wave during the 20-minute interval is likely to be twice the significant wave height, and higher still over a longer interval. The *Discovery*, using the new wave recorder south of Africa in much the same weather conditions as those experienced by HMS *Challenger*, found significant wave heights of 30 feet on several occasions and maxima of 60–70 feet.

The US satellite named Seasat which operated in the southern winter of 1978 measured surface roughness and allowed reliable estimates of wind strength and wave height. It showed that significant wave heights of 33–36 feet occurred in some part or other of the circumpolar ocean every few days, and swell almost as high. The French and US scientists who analysed the data found, contrary to earlier conclusions, that the waves in the circumpolar ocean were larger than those measured by similar methods in the north Atlantic Ocean, and attribute the difference to stronger wind in great unbounded expanses. It is, however, not true to think of wind and waves travelling uninterruptedly towards the east; the wind alternates between north-west as a depression approaches and south-west as it passes, and the waves run in much the same directions as the winds. The satellite measurements show that the highest waves occur in patches, related as one would expect to the weather patterns, though there is usually a 10 to 20 feet swell. The worst conditions have been found south of the Indian Ocean, particularly south-west of Australia. The wave maps in the Soviet Antarctic atlas are based on predictions using modern methods and recent wind studies. They indicate that the maximum wave height in the west wind region is likely to be 80 feet, and possibly 100 feet in the Indian sector near Kerguelen. These figures seem reasonable when compared with predictions of extreme conditions in the north Atlantic and Pacific Oceans. The Soviet maps show that swell higher than 13 feet is likely to be present for 30 to 70 per cent of the time between 50° S and 60° S, the Indian and Pacific sectors being the worst affected.

Work at the Admiralty Research Laboratory in 1944 showed that waves in a storm area behave as if composed of a large number of simple wave trains – a spectrum – ranging from ripples to a maximum wavelength that depends on the greatest strength of the wind, with each wave train travelling independently of the others at a speed proportional to the square root of its wavelength. The longest waves are the first to arrive at a distant coast, followed by the others in order of decreasing wavelength. Knowing the speeds of the different wavelengths and measuring their times of arrival, the distance of the coast from their common origin could be calculated and related to that of storms shown on the preceding meteorological charts. One of the remarkable discoveries was that swell from a storm near Cape Horn reached the coast of Cornwall after travelling 7000 miles in nine days, though by this time it was only 12 inches high. Some years later Walter Munk and his colleagues installed wave recorders throughout the whole length of the Pacific Ocean and studied the changes in swell as it travelled from New Zealand to Alaska.

Swell from the circumpolar ocean produces much surf on Southern Hemisphere beaches. By the time it gets there separation of the long and short wavelengths results in narrowing of the range of wavelengths arriving at any one time, conditions that are favourable to regular alternation of high and low groups of waves. Further analysis of such conditions, well supported by observations, shows that one wave in 23 is likely to be twice the average height, and one in 1173 three times the average height. It is remarkable how many anglers fishing from the rocks off southern continents are taken unawares by occasional inevitably high waves. The waves and swell are not so high round the Antarctic continent, though often enough to make boat landings difficult. Although the east winds are sometimes strong, the eastward movement of the atmospheric depressions generally means that they have a briefer and less extensive effect on the water. There is also sheltering by ice.

The sea floor Similarity between the shape of the east coast of North and South America and that of the west coast of Europe and Africa made early scientists, including Francis Bacon, speculate on the possibility that they were once joined together. It became more exciting when similarities were also found between rocks, fauna and flora, and the run of mountain chains. In the middle of the nineteenth century it was suggested that all the continents had been joined. A more definite proposal was put forward early this century by Edward Suess who, finding similar rocks, coal measures, glacial deposits and a genus of fossil plants, *Glossopteris*, in India, Australia, South America and South Africa, believed they had been united with Antarctica in a single continent which he named Gondwanaland, after a historic province of central India where he first studied the memorable rock series. Hartley T. Ferrar, on Scott's first expedition was the first to find *Glossopteris* in Antarctica, at the head of the glacier that bears his name. Edward Wilson found it in the cliffs of Mt Buckley by the side of the Beardmore glacier and carried it to their last camp.

A wealth of geological evidence supporting the Gondwanaland hypothesis, and suggesting that the supercontinent drifted in the south polar region before separating into several parts was published in 1937 by Alexander Du Toit in his book *Our Wandering Continents* dedicated to Alfred Wegener, who had earlier published a theory of continental drift based largely on the close match of the Atlantic coasts of South America and Africa. The idea has always been controversial and geophysicists, who could not envisage a source of energy sufficient to move the continents, did not take it very seriously till the 1960s.

Studies of the oceans and observations at sea provided fresh inspiration. It was recognized that submarine earthquakes are concentrated along mid-ocean ridges as well as some continental margins; measurements of the outward flow of heat through the earth's crust give higher figures over the ridges, and the ridges have active volcanoes. Along the crest of a mid-ocean ridge there is typically a submarine valley floored with highly magnetized, newly formed basalt, and magnetic surveys, with towed magnetometers and from the air, show characteristic linear magnetic anomalies paralleling the ridges symmetrically on both sides. The worldwide correlation of such anomalies and their spacings provides convincing evidence that they result from reversals of the earth's magnetism, each parallel strip showing the direction of magnetization during the period in which it was being formed.

The conclusion that the mid-ocean ridges are geologically speaking rather recent, is also supported by the finding of relatively thin layers of sediment near the ridges and thickening layers towards the continents.

Dredging, coring and the US deep drilling in the south Atlantic Ocean have led to the conclusion that its deep floor has been formed by spreading from the mid-ocean ridge during the past 65 million years, and confirmed the assumptions made in assigning provisional ages to the parallel strips of magnetic anomaly. The rate of spreading, to east and west, is estimated at 2 cm a year. The parallel magnetic anomalies are sometimes found to be offset where the ridge appears to have undergone lateral displacement; the existence of such large-scale fractures affords further evidence of active sea-floor movements.

There are still many differences of opinion about the size and shape of Gondwanaland, especially about the details of separation of the new continents, but the overall idea is generally accepted. The evidence is interpreted as showing that the temperature difference between the equator and the pole was less than it is today, but the separation of the continents and development of the circumpolar ocean led, some 30 million years ago, to a cool climate in Antarctica and advancing glaciation. US scientists have found several sites, especially in the Transantarctic Mountains that run southwards from South Victoria Land, where the remains of trees as well as ferns and giant mosses indicate early vegetation dating back some 400 million years. The British Antarctic Survey has found similar evidence round the Antarctic Peninsula as far south as Alexander I Island. The vegetation is thought to have reached its climax some 80 to 90 million years ago when the finds near the peninsula indicate vegetation resembling the forests of southern Chile. The advancing glaciation, believed to be related to the development of the cold circumpolar current, probably reached its climax some 5 million years ago with an ocean circulation much as we know it today, though with an extended ice cap and the Antarctic convergence several degrees farther north. It is thought that the changes in climate are more likely to be due to the changes in distribution of the land masses than change in the amount of radiation received from the sun.

Recent studies of the sediments confirm those of Phillippi in the *Gauss*. Just north of the Antarctic convergence, diatom ooze, a siliceous deposit typical of the Antarctic region, is found covered by globigerina ooze, a calcareous deposit typical of the warmer water farther north, and near the continent diatom ooze is found above terrigenous deposits laid down when the ice was farther north. As mentioned earlier, comparison of today's sea surface temperatures with those of James Clark Ross gives a clear indication that there has been little change during the past 150 years. The recent deep drilling programme has done much to stimulate interest in relationships between topography, currents and sediments.

Topography of the sea floor   Except for the deep embayments of the Ross and Weddell Seas the Antarctic continent has mostly a narrow continental shelf, and everywhere the shelf is at least twice as deep as those of other continents except Greenland – the other one with a large ice cap. A ship sailing southwards generally finds its soundings rising from abyssal depths to less than 500 m on an outer bank before deepening again to about 1000 m, and in some places more, in a shelf basin. The early scientists believed the shelf basins to be almost continuously peripheral to the continent like a moat, and either supposed the outer bank to be a moraine belonging to a previous ice age, or the trough to be caused by cracking when the continent was sinking under the great weight of ice. The new wealth of soundings gives a more complex picture in which the basins are often separated by ridges extending radially from the continent, and the outer bank breached by deep channels, some of them shown to be submarine canyons, scoured by outward transport of water laden with dense bottom material. There are, however, enough deeps to give a collective picture of peripheral troughs, some of them extending below continental ice shelves that reach out to sea, and of extensive outer banks, now generally believed to be composed of morainic material, though not studied as closely as might be expected.

145

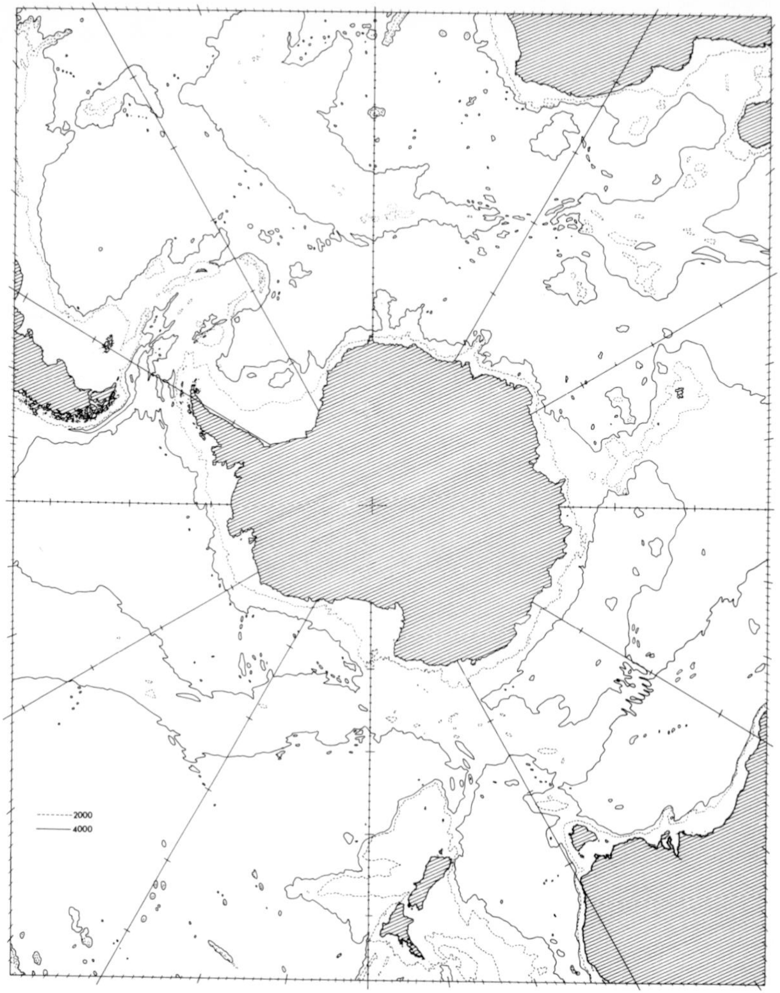

Figure 37
The 2000 and 4000 m sea-floor contours (after
the USSR 1974 bathymetric chart)

The deep ocean outside the continental shelf is mostly more than 4000 m deep and much of it between 5000 and 6000 m. The main interruptions are the Scotia Arc, the submarine ridge that joins Cape Horn through South Georgia, the South Sandwich Islands and the South Orkney Islands to the Antarctic Peninsula, and complex ridge systems linking Tasmania and New Zealand to the Balleny Islands and the continent. There is also a significant obstruction where the Kerguelen plateau extends south-east through Heard Island leaving only a narrow channel with depths greater than 3000 m between the plateau and the continent. There are several radial ridges extending 200 to 300 miles northwards from the continental shelf south of Africa.

The outline bathymetric map in Figure 37 shows the Mid-Atlantic Ridge bending east midway between South Africa and Antarctica to the Marion–Crozet plateau and then north-east to join the Mid-Indian Ocean Ridge in about 26° S. The Mid-Indian Ocean Ridge runs south-east to Amsterdam and St Paul Islands and then mainly east midway between Australia and the Antarctic continent till it reaches the region of complex topography south of Tasmania and New Zealand. A well-defined ridge joins this area to the Mid-Pacific Ocean Ridge in 50° S, and this mid-ocean ridge is linked to South America by another, branching off in 35° S and reaching the coast of Chile in 45° S.

The closer the pattern of soundings the more rugged the topography of the ridges is found to be, and all the depth variations cannot be shown on a map of reasonable size. One type of map is an outline like that of Figure 37, which gives no information about the roughness but tries to show where greater depths might allow water through or higher relief obstruct its flow. Another approach uses an almost schematic or symbolic roughness accentuating the faults and fractures. The mid-

147

ocean ridges tend to isolate the deep basins round the Antarctic continent from those farther north, the main channels for northward flow of bottom water being the west Atlantic basin, a gap between the Crozet and Kerguelen plateaus, and the east Pacific basin. There is, for example, a sharp difference in bottom temperature between the two sides of the ridge south of Australia; only a little cold water gets through the gap or fracture zone in 120° E to 127° E. Theoretical considerations require that the circumpolar current will be deflected to the north as it enters shallowing soundings and to the south as the depth increases. Such deflections seem to take place as the current approaches and leaves the Kerguelen plateau, and there is a remarkable northward advance of cold water as it approaches the ridge in the west Pacific sector. The S-shape bend in both the current and the Antarctic convergence between the Falkland Islands and South Georgia is almost certainly due to the northern arm of the Scotia Arc.

The floors of the deep ocean basins are generally very flat, the minor irregularities being smoothed over by sand and mud carried by bottom currents from the neighbouring continents, and by remains of plant and animal life raining down from above, but the closer soundings of recent years begin to reveal more local features, often with evidence of volcanic activity. The sediments are related to the water types and typical flora and fauna. The proportions of siliceous and calcareous sediments vary over several degrees of latitude near the Antarctic convergence, and farther north the calcium content depends on the temperature and carbon-dioxide content of the Antarctic bottom water as well as the depth. Most of the glacial material from the Antarctic continent is believed to be deposited within 10 degrees of latitude from the coast. Study of the heavy minerals in the sediments has provided much information about the continental rocks; the *Challenger* finds included glauconite which is typical of continental margins. Different thicknesses of sediment have been related to the currents and topography.

Manganese nodules have been found in many places; they are formed by manganese and iron separating from the water, and, instead of settling as particles, aggregating round nuclei of other materials, or as coatings on rock. They contain small, varying, amounts of nickel and cobalt that may make them valuable enough for commercial exploitation. The high oxygen content of the Antarctic bottom water probably assists in their formation.

The most recent depth chart was published by the Canadian Hydrographic Service in 1980, in continuation of the *General Bathymetric Chart of the Oceans* series established by Prince Albert I of Monaco in 1903, but although ideal for the continental shelf, nine sheets are needed to cover the whole of the circumpolar ocean. For general use the *Antarctic Bathymetric Chart* published in 1974 by the Office of Geodesy and Cartography in Moscow is more convenient. There are also good maps in the Soviet World and Antarctic atlases. The physiographic diagram in the new, 1981, National Geographic atlas seems to impose too much symbolic roughness on the submarine ridges.

Productivity

In contrast to the barren and hostile continent the surrounding ocean is bountiful though not uniformly rich. The summer productive season lasts only about four months, and less in high latitudes where the ice cover lingers, and there is richer phytoplankton growth in coastal and ice-edge regions than in the open ocean. Nevertheless rich populations

149

of seals, penguins and other birds, krill, squid and fish, and the former abundance of whales show its fertility. Primary growth, that of the phytoplankton, the microscopic unicellular plants, depends on the supply of nutrients such as phosphate, nitrate and silicate, and on the presence of adequate sunlight. South of the Antarctic convergence it seems very unlikely that growth is ever limited by shortage of nutrients, and sunlight must be the main controlling factor, not only its strength in well-illuminated near-surface depths, but also the time the plants, being stirred up and down by wind and wave action, remain near enough to the surface to enjoy sufficient light to promote growth and reproduction.

The circumpolar ocean is particularly rich in nutrients because they are supplied by deep currents which become richer as they go along since the nutrients taken from the water in the photosynthetic zone near the surface, and used by the plants and animals, are largely regenerated by decay in the deep levels. The deep currents approaching the circumpolar ocean from the north are further enriched by mixing with the nutrient-rich waters of the Antarctic intermediate and bottom currents. In spite of considerable losses to the north in these currents, the circumpolar deep-water flow becomes richer towards the east, and its northward branches in the Indian and Pacific Oceans also enrich as they go so that the nutrient concentrations in the north Pacific Ocean are about three times as large as those of the north Atlantic Ocean where perhaps a fifth of the flow started.

Phosphate and nitrate are most abundant in the upper, maximum-temperature part of the warm deep water, probably because most of their regeneration seems likely to take place between the Antarctic surface and intermediate waters sinking to the north and the warm water climbing to the south below them. The silicate concentration is greatest in the deeper boundary layer between deep and bottom waters, indicating that the regeneration and recycling of silicate takes place at a greater depth than phosphate and nitrate. The rich nutrients of the deep currents are passed on to the surface water by vertical mixing, especially far south where the interchanges are most active, but also fairly generally, since the vertical density gradients between the surface, deep and bottom layers are relatively weak.

The nutrient levels of the near-surface water are reduced by spring and summer growth, but they are sufficient, or renewed quickly enough by mixing with underlying water, to resist depletion to levels likely to limit growth. In the northern part of the Antarctic zone phytoplankton growth is richest in December, a month or so later farther south, and even later in areas that have remained covered with heavy ice. Herbivorous species of zooplankton reach their maximum a month or so after the phytoplankton, and carnivores increase less rapidly and remain abundant for a longer period. As early as 1935 H. H. Gran and T. Braarud of the University of Oslo showed that in turbulent waters the phytoplankton is more or less evenly distributed from the surface downwards as far as the water has been thoroughly mixed. This meant that some of it had been carried below the level where there was enough light to sustain photosynthesis and propagation. There has been too little detailed physical and biological investigation of well-mixed surface layers to assess the overall effect of downward mixing, but there is no doubt of the beneficial effect of increased stability of the near-surface water near land and melting ice. Far from the land and melting ice the Antarctic ocean is usually blue or grey but near them it changes to green. The winter ice edge is a desolate place.

Circumpolarity The records and collections of the early expeditions gave a clear indication that the Antarctic and subantarctic phytoplankton and zooplankton species are circumpolar in distribution, the same species being encountered in any longitude. This was confirmed by the Discovery surveys which were circumpolar and lasted long enough to eliminate possible misinterpretations due to the samples being collected in different seasons. Only two exceptions are known, a high-latitude salp and a subantarctic lantern fish, which have been found only in the Pacific sector. There are examples in which the circumpolar distribution is not uniform. *Euphausia superba*, for example, is circumpolar in the East Wind Drift, but its abundance in the West Wind Drift seems to depend largely on northern outflow from the east wind region, which is concentrated in some areas. J. P. Kennett has shown that Antarctic and subantarctic microfossil assemblages are circumpolar in the deep-sea sediments.

Bottom-living organisms, especially those of shallow, near-coastal waters seem to range less widely; although they are influenced in general by the circumpolar currents, various authors have distinguished sub-regions or provinces linked to different parts of the continent or to Antarctic and subantarctic islands, from which different species are believed to spread along relatively shallow underwater connections. Deeper-living bottom dwellers have not been studied as comprehensively as the plankton but it seems that their distributions may be more closely related to the currents than to land connections. The littoral flora and fauna of the continent and nearby islands tends to be destroyed down to a depth of 10 to 20 m by moving ice or ground ice, but even this vulnerable zone swarms with active bottom-living organisms during the summer.

North to south zonation   The Discovery surveys showed that nearly every upper-layer plankton species belongs to a characteristic circumpolar zone, many Antarctic species, for example, extending up to, but only occasionally beyond, the Antarctic convergence, and patterns of this kind observed in one sector of the ocean hold good in others. A. de C. Baker studying the north to south distribution of *Euphausia* species in the central Indian Ocean found that 8 of the 15 species are restricted to a greater or lesser extent by the Antarctic and subtropical convergences. C. Tate Regan studying the fishes of Scott's last expedition found them subdivided into species typical of each of three zones, Antarctic, subantarctic and subtropical, with the 6 and 12 °C isotherms as approximate boundaries. J. R. Norman, working on the *Discovery* fishes confirmed this zonation and pointed out that the 6 and 12 °C isotherms correspond closely to the convergences that demarcate different water circulations.

P. M. David found that a commonly occurring chaetognath *Sagitta gazellae* has two distinguishable races, the population north of the Antarctic convergence maturing at a shorter length than the Antarctic population. One of the most abundant copepods, *Calanoides acutus*, lives mainly south of the Antarctic convergence, with only a limited extension into the deeper levels of the subantarctic zone to which it may be carried by the sinking Antarctic water. Many similar examples can be found in the *Discovery Reports*, as well as examples of species whose north to south distributions are not influenced by the changes in water conditions across the convergence. T. J. Hart, studying phytoplankton distributions, found a number of species typical of the Antarctic, subantarctic and subtropical regions. He noted that *Rhizosolenia curvata* is a good indicator of subantarctic water when it is carried southwards over Antarctic water; it lives for a time, but rarity of large individuals such as result from normal growth indicates that it cannot survive for long in its new, rapidly changing, environment.

A recent summary by J. P. Kennett shows the Antarctic convergence as an important biogeographical boundary for foraminifera, radiolaria and pteropods, in the surface plankton as well as their microfossils on the sea bed. Difficulty in getting echo soundings in the early days, when the sound source was not very powerful and the operator had to listen for the echo, was attributed to the possibility of an accumulation of soft sediment near the convergence, and this seems to be supported by reports from the deep-drilling ship *Glomar Challenger* of an anomalously thick layer of acoustically transparent sediment just south of the convergence; it might have been a fairly good absorber for the weak sound beams.

There is also evidence of some zooplankton species being more abundant and others less abundant near the Antarctic convergence, possibly because of special conditions prevailing there. David found poor catches of *Sagitta gazellae* near the convergence, contrasting with richer catches north and south of it, and J. E. Kane found a low-concentration belt of *Parathemisto* near the convergence. In contrast Baker found *Euphausia triacantha* most abundant there, the numbers decreasing rapidly on both sides.

Farther north, the fragments of subantarctic front as recognized by Böhnecke, Burling and others seem also to have biogeographical significance, some plankton species occurring mainly in the warmer, stratified, northern half of the subantarctic zone and others in the well-mixed water of the southern half. Baker found the southern region to be the normal habitat of *Euphausia triacantha* and K. J. H. Andrews found the same for *Calanoides acutus*. D. D. John and Baker found

Euphausia vallentini to be restricted to the cooler belt, and other Euphausian species to the warmer half. There are greater differences between the two sides of the subtropical convergence which marks the southern limit of distribution of many warm-water species.

Temperature and salinity have been supposed to be the most influential factors controlling biological distributions in the ocean, but they are themselves largely dependent on water movements, typically on current branches and partly closed horizontal and vertical circulations that maintain a fairly narrow range of conditions. In the Antarctic ocean especially, water movements may have very different histories, routes and travel times without acquiring very different temperatures and salinities, and it may be the circulations, especially if they are likely to favour migrations between ideal breeding and feeding grounds, that are of most basic importance.

Many zooplankton species make vertical movements of their own. Net hauls at different depths show that there are more zooplankton near the surface at night and fewer at 100 to 200 m, and the opposite happens during the day. This migration is very apparent on modern echo-sounding records; echoes from different plankton species and predators feeding on them show as a broad band of mid-water echoes that climb nearer the surface as the sun goes down. As the sun rises the echo layer, commonly named the deep scattering layer, sinks again to its daytime level, sometimes showing some stratification. Not all the species take part, and the reason for the migration is not fully understood, but it is generally associated with changes in light intensity, the species involved tending to seek levels of illumination to which they are adapted. There is some evidence that the movements are lessened by bright moonlight, and that they respond to solar eclipses. There is also

Figure 38
Wandering Albatross on nest, Undine Harbour,
South Georgia, 23 November 1929

evidence that they are lessened in the continuing summer daylight of the polar sea. Vertical movement as the light changes may be partly related to feeding and avoidance of predators; herbivores have to spend some time near the surface where the phytoplankton is most abundant, and while the darkness will not reduce the efficiency of their own filtering mechanisms it might make them less vulnerable to predators; sinking and being more spread out over a larger vertical range may be beneficial in daylight.

Many of the Antarctic zooplankton species that inhabit the surface layer in summer go down to the warm deep water in winter. Nets fished horizontally at depths down to 1000 m show that in summer the zooplankton population of the first 100 m is larger than that of the deep water, but in winter the catches are smaller near the surface and greater in the deep water. It is a much more extended migration than the diurnal migration and we can only guess its cause and effect; the herbivores have less to gain by coming to the surface in winter when the phytoplankton is scarce and they may be safer spread out over a greater vertical range in the deep water than in a narrower range near the surface where the birds as well as other predators can take their toll. The up and down movement between the southward moving deep water and the northward moving surface water might help to maintain a particular population within its optimum geographic range. Not all the zooplankton species take part in this deep migration, notably the particularly important *Euphausia superba*. For most species there is evidence that although the bulk of the population migrates downwards in winter there are always some left near the surface. Perhaps there is always some traffic between the surface and deep layers. Some species migrate diurnally and not seasonally; others do both.

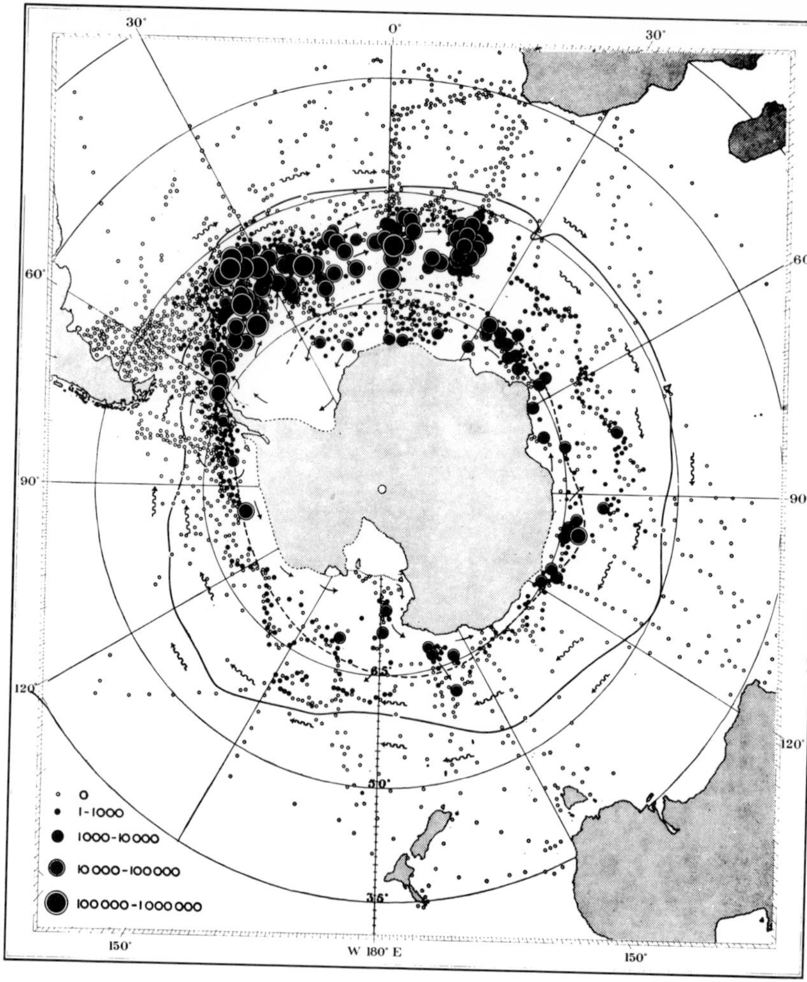

Figure 39
The circumpolar distribution of *Euphausia
superba* (krill) including the later larval stages,
adolescents and adults. (Figure 143 of Natural
History and Geography of the Antarctic Krill,
Discovery Report, Volume 32, 1962, by James
Marr)

Krill The distribution of *Euphausia superba*, the main food of the baleen whales, the Crab-eater seals, penguins and other birds, fish and squid, seems very dependent on the water movements. The largest populations are found near the continental slope of Antarctica and in areas manifestly enriched by northward outflows from the near-continental east wind region. Figure 39 taken from James Marr's *Natural History and Geography of the Antarctic Krill* shows his map of its overall abundance. He found the largest concentrations in the current flowing from the Weddell Sea, particularly near the South Shetland Islands and South Georgia, but believed that his diagram probably minimized the populations near the continent where they could not be sampled so frequently, and only during the summer. Marr was more concerned with careful presentation of all the evidence, and pointing out where more observations are required, than with advancing any particular explanation, but his comprehensive analysis and the studies of later workers give a clear indication that the richest regions are those whose water movements seem to make them most favourable to the hatching of the eggs and survival of the early larval stages, and those to which the later larval stages are directly transported by surface currents.

Females with eggs are found over the whole range of distribution near the surface, but the eggs sink rapidly. Near the continental slope the eggs are taken mainly in nets fished below 1000 m, or close to the bottom in shallower water. Farther north, near South Georgia, sufficient nets have been fished at depths down to 1000 m, and a rather less convincing number at 1500 m or very close to the bottom, to show that hatching, if it occurs there at all, must take place at still greater depths. If the eggs did not sink rapidly few would be likely to survive the remarkably efficient collecting and filtering mechanisms that the krill use in feeding on the

159

Figure 40
Fishing for larval krill in the Weddell Sea,
18 March 1937. James Marr is the middle
figure at the ship's rail

phytoplankton, and the nets fished at shallow depths at the right time of year would have caught them. The eggs laid by a single female are directed away from her feeding mechanism, but if laid in a mixed swarm they seem likely to be vulnerable.

The eggs develop as they sink, and after hatching the early larvae rise towards the surface, passing through three recognizable stages at successively higher levels till the fourth, named the first calyptopis, which needs to feed on phytoplankton, arrives near the surface. The whole development, from spawning of the eggs to arrival of the first calyptopis at its shallow feeding place takes only a month, and it is reasonable to suppose that this is accomplished more successfully in some regions than in others. It may be easier near the continental slope where the eggs may not sink very deep and there are likely to be rising as well as sinking water movements. There may also be favourable conditions in the well-mixed water in the sharp current boundary between Weddell Sea and Drake Passage waters near the South Shetland Islands and the South Orkneys, and perhaps in the Weddell Sea current, and between it and neighbouring warmer waters farther east across the Atlantic sector. Near South Georgia, where relatively warm water extends to great depths, the eggs may sink too deep to allow successful larval ascent. It seems quite possible that although krill grow to their largest size and can be very abundant near the northern limits of their distribution, reproduction is not successful there, and the populations have to be maintained by transport of larvae from more successful breeding grounds farther south. The growing threat of commercial exploitation makes it important that such questions should be settled.

One of the most remarkable features of the circumpolar krill

162

distribution, very noticeable in Figure 39, is the sharp fall in abundance from west to east in 30° E. It seems anomalous that the Weddell Sea current, which can be distinguished in the temperature and ice charts as far as 30° E, and is rich in advanced krill larvae at the end of winter, should not promote the same richness farther east. It prompts the suggestion that the krill might migrate or be carried southwards and enrich the coastal region, making up to some extent for the vast outpouring that seems to take place farther west. There seems, however, to be no indisputable evidence of southward flow in the surface layer where the krill live. The ice edge bends southwards in summer but mainly because the Weddell Sea ice tongue maintains the northern boundary west of 30° E; in winter there is no sharp southward bend, only the gradual circumpolar trend. There are clear indications of a stronger than usual southward movement in the warm deep layer, but once the krill reach the surface layer they seem to remain there; they do not migrate down to the warm deep layer in winter like many other zooplankton species.

Near to the continent, the southward Ekman transport and the southward trend at the surface due to the effect of the earth's rotation on the westward flow may be partly responsible for keeping the krill within what seems to be their most favourable habitat near the continental slope. They may move on their own; Japanese scientists tracked swarms travelling irregularly southwards at about 6·5 miles a day in the east wind region off Enderby Land while neighbouring icebergs were moving north-west.

Krill do not, however, seem to penetrate far south on the continental shelf. Marr's study of the Ross Sea showed that although they are abundant in the deep water to the north, only a few larvae and early

Figure 41
Lincoln Ellsworth's ship *Wyatt Earp* moored to fast ice in the Bay of Whales; part of the Ross Ice Shelf can be seen in the middle background to the right, 21 January 1936

163

stages were found on the shelf. Proximity of the warm deep water seems to be important; although eggs and early larval stages are found in cold shelf water in the Bransfield Strait the deep water is not far away, and most of them and the adult krill are found on the fringes of the warm deep current along the southern shores of the South Shetland Islands as well as outside the strait. In contrast, another euphausian, *E. crystallorophias*, spawns and lives close inshore, the different distributions of the two species probably being related to their different reproductive programmes. The Ross Sea whaling was conducted mainly outside the shelf sea in the deep water where *E. superba* is plentiful, but there were many small whales near the ice shelf, presumably feeding on *E. crystallorophias*. R. M. Laws has pointed out that Crab-eater Seals which live mainly on *E. superba* are relatively scarce in the Ross Sea.

There are so many reports of the abundance of krill in and near pack ice all round the circumpolar ocean that they have been regarded as 'creatures of the ice', but their presence near ice is probably only incidental to them being creatures of the near-coastal East Wind Drift and its northward branches, particularly the Weddell Sea current, that carry ice as well as krill. In the Bouvet region krill are encountered at the ice edge, but the ice is so far north only because it is carried by the current that carries the krill, and still carries them after the ice has melted. Where the krill extend far north as they do north and west of South Georgia they are likely to be encountered well to the north of the ice edge, and where their northern limit is far south, as it is south of eastern Australia, a winter observer reaches the ice edge and finds no krill.

Relating krill abundance to the cold currents rather than the ice does not contradict the old picture of whalers pushing southwards to the ice, or their generalization that the number of whales near South Georgia varied with the proximity of the ice. In cold years like 1927–28 and 1930–31 the Discovery surveys showed krill catches considerably higher than the overall mean, while in 1936–37 which was a warm year the catches were considerably less. Nor does it upset the early finding of a correlation between the distribution of whale captures near South Georgia and that of phosphate in the water. The Weddell Sea current brings higher phosphate concentrations as well as more krill.

Climate One of the remarkable characteristics of the circumpolar ocean is the smallness of difference of water temperature between winter and summer, the difference between the means for the coldest and warmest months being less than 2 °C over most of the ocean south of 60° S and not more than 5 °C round its northern fringe. The latitudinal stability of the wind and current means is also remarkable. The west to east tracks of the cyclonic atmospheric disturbances vary considerably but not as much as those of the Northern Hemisphere. Winter and summer mean air temperatures vary much the same as the sea surface temperatures except close to the continent and within the winter sea-ice cover where the annual variation is generally 20 °C or more and there are large day to day variations as the wind comes from north or south. Edmond Halley and the early explorers who followed him were surprised at the coldness of summer weather in the circumpolar ocean compared with that in similar and even higher latitudes in the Northern Hemisphere. This must be largely due to the very small proportion of land in 40° S to 60° S compared with corresponding northern latitudes, and the effect of the relatively cold continuous circumpolar flow. The atlas of zonal mean

Figure 42
Thawing out of blocks and flexible drives with
paraffin flares, 68° S 79° W, 10 March 1934

wind speeds published by the US National Center for Atmospheric Research shows that very strong mean winds, 30 to 45 knots, are more widespread round the ocean in summer than in winter. The early explorers found that the barometer stood, on average, 1 inch lower than in corresponding northern latitudes.

D. D. John describing the 1932 circumpolar voyage of the *Discovery II* to the Royal Geographical Society said 'Some of us with the experience of several summer seasons elsewhere in the Antarctic had supposed that these winter cruises would be so rigorous as to be extremely unpleasant. It was not altogether so. The conditions were of course harder than those of summer. If there was a gale with heavy seas and spray the ship's decks and bulwarks and upper works became thickly encrusted with ice. Ropes and wires and shrouds became enormous and beautiful. We found difficulty in working our gear on stations at the lowest temperatures. The blocks and sheaves over which ran the wires, lowering the nets and instruments into the sea, became seized up with ice and had to be thawed out with flaming torches of burning waste and paraffin before a station could be started.' He went on to describe the difficulty of keeping ice out of the water-sampling instruments and the beauties of the Aurora Australis which was such a feature of the winter nights south of Australia and New Zealand. E. W. Nelson had still more difficulty with his sampling in McMurdo Sound: he had to take a pick and shovel to re-open the hole in the ice every time.

D. D. John in his lecture to the Royal Geographical Society also emphasized the bearing of the Antarctic convergence on climate. 'It is a physical boundary very easily and precisely detected with a thermometer by the sharp change in temperature as one passes from one zone to another. It can be detected as easily if not so precisely by a zoologist with a tow-net, because each of the two waters has a distinctive fauna of floating animal life. The zoologist need only know the species of prawns of the genus *Euphausia* to which *Euphausia superba*, whale-food, belongs. They are so numerous in the surface that his net will always catch some. If, in the neighbourhood of the convergence, he takes *Euphausia vallentini* or *Euphausia longirostris* he is in sub-Antarctic water. He will have crossed the convergence and be in the Antarctic when his net brings back *Euphausia frigida* and not *vallentini* nor *longirostris*. But we, whether sailors or scientists, know and will remember the convergence best in another way: as the line to the north of which we felt one day, at the right season, after months in the Antarctic, genial air again and soft rain like English rain in the spring. I can remember a number of those days vividly. It was like passing at one step from winter to spring. In the southernmost lands in the sub-Antarctic, the islands about Cape Horn, the earth smells as earth should smell and as it never does in the Antarctic. It is no doubt the north-easterly course of the convergence between the longitudes of Cape Horn and South Georgia, so that the former is left far to the north and the latter to the south, that accounts for the vast difference in the climates of two islands which are in precisely the same latitude and only 1000 miles apart. The lower slopes of Staten Island are clothed with beech trees with so rich an undergrowth that it is difficult to push through. Darwin compared the richness of the region to that of a tropical forest. South Georgia, the other island, is a true Antarctic land. The snow-line of South Georgia is lower than the tree-line of Tierra del Fuego.'

It is difficult to make detailed comparisons of island sea and air temperatures because of the scarcity of sea data, but the charts of mean temperature show that they are within about 1 °C of each other, the air tending to be warmer than the water in spring and early summer, and the water being warmer in autumn and winter. Kerguelen and Heard Islands, only 200 miles apart but on opposite sides of the convergence have mean annual air temperatures of 4·3 °C and 1·1 °C. Macquarie Island just north of the convergence has a mean temperature of 4·5 °C. The ships of the Discovery Investigations made sufficient surveys of the ocean round South Georgia to show that its year to year changes in mean annual air temperature followed those of the water very closely. Air temperatures are available since 1905; between 1950 and 1981 the mean annual temperature ranged from 0·8 to 2·6 °C with an average of 2·0 °C. During the previous thirty years it ranged from 0·6 to 2·6 °C but with an average of only 1·5 °C. We do not know whether the recent warming will last; an earlier average between 1905 and 1910 was 2·1 °C though perhaps biased a little by fewer night time readings.

Tides   In the early 1830s it was supposed that the circumpolar ocean, the only continuous belt of water encircling the earth, must be the main source of the world's tides. It was supposed that there must be two primary tidal waves travelling round it, 180 degrees of longitude apart, keeping pace with the moon, and sending secondary waves northwards into the Atlantic, Indian and Pacific Oceans. The idea did not last long, because it was too difficult to see how a long wave, whose speed is controlled mainly by the depth of water, could travel so fast. Also as more tidal observations were made along the coasts of South America and South Africa, largely by Fitzroy in the *Beagle*, it was soon apparent that they did not fit the simple pattern of a wave travelling northwards. It was not, however, till early this century that R. A. Harris of the US Coast and

Geodetic Survey introduced the modern concept (partly suggested by Fitzroy) of the worldwide ocean subdividing itself into portions whose natural periods of oscillation match those of the tide-raising forces, and interact in a complex but regulated way with adjoining areas.

Many useful tide recordings have been made under very difficult conditions near the Antarctic coast, usually by recording the up and down movements of the ship or ice with the help of a wire anchored to the bottom, and, more recently, using a sensitive gravimeter. The British Antarctic Survey has nine years of records from the western side of the Antarctic Peninsula. US scientists secured a month's records from three pressure-measuring capsules laid on the sea floor between Australia and Antarctica, and US and Norwegian scientists have recorded tidal streams and currents in the southern and northern parts of the Weddell Sea. There are also a growing number of current recordings in the Drake Passage and south of New Zealand. Even so it will take a long time to build up a picture of the main tidal movements and their effects on the neighbouring oceans. It may have to wait for plotting of the surface topography by satellite radar altimeters, now in its early stages. Near the Antarctic coast there seems to be a general tendency for one of the semi-diurnal tides to be much larger than the other, as E. W. Nelson found on Scott's last expedition, and which he related to the moon being north or south of the equator. The effect of the earth's rotation and the north to south changes of depth near the continent also give rise to horizontal oscillatory movements in the prevailing westward current.

Conservation   The Antarctic Treaty signed by 12 countries in 1959 was concerned mainly with de-militarization of the region south of 60° S, its use for peaceful purposes, cooperation in scientific investigation, protection of its environment and prohibition of nuclear explosions and waste disposal. It included measures for conserving the flora and fauna, and in 1972 there was further agreement on the conservation of seals. In 1980 fifteen countries signed a Convention on the Conservation of Antarctic Marine Living Resources. It applies to waters south of agreed limits that approximate to the Antarctic convergence, but with a northward extension to include Marion Island, the Crozet Islands and Kerguelen. Its object includes the principle of rational use, implying that the living resources must not be harvested beyond levels that are sufficient to maintain maximum productivity, and ensure no damage to dependent or related species. It requires cooperation in collecting and sharing scientific and fisheries data, and it tells the government representatives to take full account of the recommendations and advice of its scientific committee.

At present, cooperative research on the living resources is coordinated mainly by an international non-governmental organization BIOMASS. Its meetings and publications are supported by grants from the International Council of Scientific Unions and its scientific committees for Antarctic and oceanic research, and also by the UN Food and Agriculture Organization. It has already made substantial contributions to the tasks of outlining key problems and arranging joint study, though it seems fair to judge that financial restraints have concentrated the work on manageable surveys and research projects that can conveniently be conducted on the way to and near existing bases, with perhaps too little effort on more widespread or long-term projects.

There have already been several informal meetings of a group of specialists on the possible environmental implications of mineral exploitation. While there are no minerals that could at present be mined economically on the continent, it is widely speculated that there is gas and oil under the continental shelf and there is some concern about what might happen.

Further reading   Many sources of further information are mentioned in the text, but detailed referencing, necessary in scientific papers, seemed less appropriate in this account meant primarily for non-specialist readers.

For more detailed studies the following are recommended. First – among the publications of the Hakluyt Society – *The Journals of Captain Cook*, edited by Professor J. C. Beaglehole, are a mine of information about the earlier voyages as well as those of Cook. The volumes on Halley's voyages, edited by N. J. W. Thrower, and Bellingshausen's voyage, edited by F. Debenham, are unique sources. James Clark Ross's *A Voyage of Discovery and Research in the Southern and Antarctic Regions*, first published in 1847 and reprinted by David & Charles in 1969, is a very accurate and observant account; his lively interest in all that was going on round him makes it very readable. H. R. Mill's *Siege of the South Pole* is a classical source of information on all the Antarctic voyages up to 1905. *The Antarctic Problem* by E. W. Hunter Christie, published in 1951, is a comprehensive and readable account of discovery and exploration in the Falkland sector. Two lists naming and giving summary details of all the ships believed and known to have sailed to Antarctic seas up to 1958 are given by Brian Roberts in the *Polar Record*, volume 9, 1958–59.

Papers by A. G. E. Jones give hard-won details of the early-nineteenth-century voyages.

The History of Modern Whaling by J. N. Tonnessen and A. O. Johnsen, an abridgement and translation of their earlier four-volume work, gives a lively account of the growth and decline of the industry. N. A. Mackintosh's *Stocks of Whales* (1965), and Nigel Bonner's *Whales* (1980) and *Seals and Man* (1982) are rewarding summaries of the science.

The *Discovery Reports*, volumes 1–37, 1929–80, formerly published by Cambridge University Press and now by the Institute of Oceanographic Sciences, contain information on most aspects of Antarctic ocean science. The absence of an overall index (now being planned) makes searching through them rather difficult, though some help can be obtained from a list of the contents of each volume and alphabetical list of authors that was issued in 1970.

Recent advances are published mainly in scientific journals such as *Deep-Sea Research*, *Journal of Physical Oceanography*, *Journal of Marine Research*, *Journal of Geophysical Research*, and *Polar Biology*. They also appear along with summary articles in collected papers like the *Antarctic Research Series* published by the American Geophysical Union for the National Science Foundation and the *Soviet Antarctic Expedition* series published in translation by Elsevier. The *Antarctic Map Folio Series*, volumes 1–19, published by the American Geographical Society under a contract with the National Science Foundation between 1964 and 1975, is an expressive summary of what is known about the ocean. Other valuable sources are *Meteorology of the Antarctic* published by the South African Weather Bureau in 1957, *Meteorology of the Southern Hemisphere* published by the American Meteorological Society in 1972, and *Climate of the Upper Air*, volumes 1–3, published by the Environmental Services Administration, USA, in 1969–71. Useful conference and symposium reports are *Antarctic Biology* (Paris) 1964, *Antarctic Oceanography* (Valparaiso) 1966, *Antarctic Ecology* (Cambridge) 1970, *Antarctic Ice and Water Masses* (Tokyo) 1971, *Polar Oceans* (Montreal) 1977, *Adaptations within Antarctic Ecosystems* (Washington) 1977 and *Antarctic Geoscience* (Madison, Wisconsin) 1982. There are also ocean chapters in *Research in the Antarctic* published by the American Association for the Advancement of Science in 1971 and in *Biogeography and Ecology in Antarctica*, edited by J. van Mieghem, P. van Oye and J. Schell and published in The Hague in 1965.

The *Antarctic Pilot* published by the UK Hydrographic Department, and the corresponding *Sailing Directories for Antarctica* of the USA Hydrographic Office contain much information about the ocean as well as all the details of coastlines and anchorages.

The *Southern Ocean Atlas* by A. L. Gordon, E. J. Molinelli and T. N. Baker, giving all the available information on temperature, salinity, oxygen and nutrient distributions at all depths in 250 maps and diagrams, is invaluable for research. It was published by the Columbia University Press in 1982; the data on which it is based are also available on magnetic tape.

West Wind Drift, 86–91
Wilkes, Charles, leader of US Exploring
    Expedition
  large collection of fishes, 31
  remarks on krill, 27

William Scoresby, research ship, Discovery
    Investigations, 68–9
winds in relation to atmospheric
    pressure, 35
Wüst, G., Antarctic bottom water, 52–3